T
OF THE
ARAB INTELLECTUAL

THE CRISIS
OF THE
ARAB INTELLECTUAL

TRADITIONALISM
OR
HISTORICISM?

by
ABDALLAH LAROUI

Translated from the French by
Diarmid Cammell

UNIVERSITY OF CALIFORNIA PRESS
Berkeley   Los Angeles   London

University of California Press
Berkeley and Los Angeles, California

University of California Press, Ltd.
London, England

NOTE: Chapter 5 was first published in a special number of *Diogène* (64, Oct.-Dec. 1958), "Nouvelle actualité du Marxisme," with contributions by T. W. Adorno, H. Marcuse, J. Hyppolite, E. J. Hobsbawm, M. Rodinson, A. Abdel Malek, K. Papaioannou, etc. The Appendix to Chapter 4 was written as a conclusion to the article "Europe" in the *Encyclopaedia Universalis*. The author wishes to thank the publishers concerned for their permission to reprint these articles.

Library of Congress Catalog Card Numbeer 74-29796
ISBN 0-520-02971-2

BY THE SAME AUTHOR:

L'idéologie arabe contemporaine. With a
preface by Maxime Rodinson. François Maspero, Paris, 1967.

L'histoire du Maghreb: un essai de synthèse.
François Maspero, Paris, 1970.

CONTENTS

PREFACE

Because this book was originally intended for Arab readers, I
confine my discussion to a specific question, one that, at the
time of writing, summed up the Arabs' search for solutions
to the problem of their historical development.

The first three chapters and the Conclusion were delivered
as public lectures at Rabat, Algiers, Tunis, and Beirut. My
audiences, largely composed of academics, were of course
familiar with recent Arab history.

This history may be divided into four principal stages:

1. The *Nahda*, a vast political and cultural movement that
dominates the period of 1850 to 1914. Originating in Syria
and flowering in Egypt, the Nahda sought through translation
and vulgarization to assimilate the great achievements of
modern European civilization, the while reviving the classical
Arab culture that antedates the centuries of decadence and
foreign domination.

2. The struggle for independence. In the principal Arab
countries this lasted from the end of the First World War to
the mid-1950s. It gave rise to popular parties that played an
important cultural role by promoting the spread of democratic ideals and, to a lesser extent, of socialist values.

3. The Unionist movement, which existed well before the
Second World War but did not make its real influence felt

until after the crisis following the loss of Palestine. Symbolized for a short period by the League of Arab States, and strengthened by the success of the Baath party in Syria and Iraq and by an increasingly lively concern with social justice and economic progress, the movement found an apologist and hero in the person of Gamal Abdul Nasser.

4. The moral crisis consequent upon the defeat of the Arab armies in the June 1967 war. This culminated in a period of anguished self-criticism, a searching reappraisal of postwar Arab culture and political practice. The principal victim of this process has been Nasserism.

There are those who maintain (a little hastily, in my opinion) that the Arabs have entered upon a new phase since the October 1973 war. Characterized by an equilibrium favorable to both the conservatives and the leftist revolutionaries, the new situation may well result in an increasingly pronounced polarization of forces.

My listeners did not need to be reminded of this historical background; rather, they were concerned to hear a discussion of the consequences and an evaluation of the dominant ideologies. What are the definitive achievements of the Nahda, the shortcomings of the traditional political parties, the causes of the relative failures of Nasserism and of Baathism, the reasons for the failure of Arab Marxism? What interested my listeners was not so much the positive results as the failures of these movements; for the question they were asking, given the situation around 1970, was this: Why, in spite of all our efforts, are we facing the same difficulties as our parents and grandparents faced?

The central thesis of this book is that the concept of history—a concept playing a capital role in "modern" thought—is in fact peripheral to all the ideologies that have dominated the Arab world till now. If this thesis can be established—it is for the reader to decide whether I have gathered sufficient evidence—what conclusions ensue? Does it follow that the renovating movements have failed because their conception of history is false? And if the answer to this question is "yes," does it follow that the Arab intellectuals have only to appreciate this point in order to find miraculous solutions to all the problems besetting their society? If in fact that were my conclusion, the diagnosis would indeed be superficial and the remedy simplistic.

To understand the historical process is to understand both oneself and others in a temporal perspective; it is to conceive of tested and effective courses of action. To the extent that Arab intellectuals, a good number of whom are also political leaders, have a non-evolutionary conception of reality, so will all collective action in the Arab milieu be deprived of a constant and definite orientation; and so will politics, in the noble sense of the word, be reduced to the level of short-sighted tactical manoeuvering subservient to egotistical interests. But it must be stressed that if the Arab intelligentsia has not succeeded in working out a theory of history but is beginning to acquire the necessary historical consciousness— a fact to which my own book, among others, bears witness— that is for well-defined, objective reasons, which I have attempted to analyze in Chapter IV. Thus my method is phenomenological, since I have undertaken to describe the historicization of at least one area of Arab thought. My aim is not so much to uncover the causes of past failures or to prescribe remedial action as to understand, through examination of a cultural fact of symbolic value, the real evolution of Arab society.

Nevertheless, in the Conclusion I call upon Arab intellectuals to espouse and propagandize an "historicist" rationale. Why do I abandon the domain of cultural society in order to launch into ideology?

When intellectuals think collectively about the failures of their society, they do so because of a belief that they can find remedies. Those who deny all effectiveness to ideas, yet who organize themselves into active groups, are living an irreducible contradiction. Having become concerned with an essentially political problem, the Arab intelligentsia must inevitably reach the stage where it passes from diagnosis of the situation to prescription of remedial action. Why should I escape from this rule? Moreover, both liberal political science and the Marxist left acknowledge the existence of a minority (which the one terms a modernizing elite and the other an avant-garde) possessing new values in whose name society is to be remodeled. The role in the Arab world of minorities, and of intellectual minorities in particular, need not be labored further, although this admission does not imply a lapse into idealism.

Finally, what of historicism itself?

Historicism, though born in Europe, has today fallen into disfavor in the industrialized West. If it were regarded as a means of analyzing the Arab world or as offering a solution to contradictions experienced by this world, such a position would be tantamount to borrowing a worn-out version of reality. This objection may be raised both by the Arab reader, concerned about originality, and the Western reader, who may dislike historicism.

I am not attempting a philosophical rehabilitation of historicism in opposition to the numerous schools that are hostile to it. What I do state is that it alone offers a rationale for collective action—and it is action with which the Arabs must be concerned. Historicism is implied therefore in all their planning. Those who criticize historicism as a philosophy—I refer in particular to the Frenchman L. Althusser—are interested primarily in a rationale of understanding: they take as models the exact sciences, which presume an eternal present and a homogeneous milieu. A society that believes itself to be at the apogee of evolution and that strives to preserve the equilibrium it imagines it has attained will experience no difficulty in transposing such a rationale to the social and human sciences. But a society that rejects its present, that lacks homogeneity, that feels itself to be different from those cultures that appear to be in the ascendant, will rediscover historicism as the theoretical justification for its course of action, sometimes in the guise of Marxism (see Chapter V).

If the reader is interested neither in such a rationale of action nor in the unequal development of nations; if he lacks belief in the effective role of the intelligentsia and thinks that progress is nothing if not the expansion of the gross national product—then he will certainly consider many of my remarks in the following pages subjective or unfounded. But the reader must remember that the Arab intellectual *is* interested in such a rationale and *does* believe in the above propositions, without even feeling the need to justify them. Then it will readily be understood that the main concern of the Arab intellectual is how to make his contribution to public life more effective. This book represents an attempt to answer this ever relevant question.

Rabat, April 1976

INTRODUCTION

The content of this book is, I quite realize, somewhat unexpected. The reality of the central fact that it attempts to elucidate can always be denied, and the very concept of cultural retardation that it is based upon can easily be rejected, for the concept is unilateral, not dialectical. Historicism, as a philosophy and a way of thinking, is as devalued as the scientism, positivism, and metaphysical materialism of the nineteenth century. The notions it makes use of—time, history, rationalism—are everywhere criticized and have lost their status as key concepts.

Moreover, the position defended here opens to the Arab intellectual who is at once revolutionary and responsible only the prospect of an educationalist's career; it does not offer solid incentives to literary or philosophical creation, nor does it incite to direct action upon the events that so deeply concern him. Creativity, as much cultural as political, must wait till later, with a sort of historical fatalism that will not be accepted—I readily admit—by those who for decades have been eagerly awaiting an "Arab springtime," an event that is today more uncertain than ever. Classical critiques directed at traditionalism, romanticism, anarchism, utopianism—all of which are berated, from a rationalist, historicist standpoint, as petit-bourgeois ideologies—cannot by themselves,

however scholarly and meticulous they may be, carry conviction to those for whom the present and the foreseeable
future are quite simply unendurable.

Besides, at first sight this position seems precarious. The
historical retardation described in these essays is defined as
relating to the liberal era that began in the second half of the
eighteenth century and came to fruition in the nineteenth; the
examples of compensation for historical retardation—modernization—that are singled out for frequent mention in the
following chapters (Germany and Russia) exemplify the
taking of this liberal European culture as the horizon of
cultural and political ambitions. Marxism itself as an ideology
and a political practice is, in the last analysis, a rationalism
(accompanied by a mere promise of eventual transcendence)
of this same liberal culture; this emerges clearly in the works
of Lukács and Gramsci, on which I draw extensively. Arab
culture both in its classical expression and in the most
influential aspect of its present-day expression is opposed in
almost every particular to liberal culture. We refer to retardation simply because we accept the principle that every culture
is the expression of a society, itself defined by its material
base, and also because we must fact the facts of colonization.
This last factor, considered as the symbol of the absolute
failure of the dominated society, impels us to assume a
cultural retardation; at this level there is no question of a
value judgment or of theoretical analysis in the proper
philosophical sense of the term. Thus we have already
committed ourselves to and given proof of our historicism
without in any way adducing reasons, and even refusing to
do so; for to accept the necessity for a theoretical foundation
is to owe allegiance to philosophy.

Today we are in a position to realize that the twentieth
century is wholly a reaction against this liberal culture, which
includes a certain classical Marxism. Liberal culture and
modern culture in general took historical time as its supreme
value as opposed to other conceptions of time (cosmic,
mythical, physical, psychological); it consequently devalued

those world views that were founded either on these other conceptions or on a relativization, a placing between parentheses, of historical time. The mythologies, the Platonically inspired philosophies, the religious ideologies, the theologies, the rational metaphysics founded upon physical time, the cyclic philosophies of history, the romantic utopias, the philosophies of art, etc., which all subordinate historical time to some higher value, are relegated to the level of unconscious discourse, though doing so entails a search for the cause of this unconsciousness in the socioeconomic structure and an attempt to isolate the "rational core" of each of them. But from the moment that reaction sets in against the primacy of time, all the above-mentioned world views rediscover their internal rationality. They return to the surface, entire or in part, in extremely subtle disguises, with outward appearances of a rigorous scientific formulation. Arab culture has participated, at every level, in each of these world views. Therefore it is not surprising if today several aspects of that culture can be revived. Far from seeming backward, they appear on the contrary to be ahead of, or at least on the same level as, modern tendencies. Let us take a quick look at some examples in order to verify how easy it is to support this assertion.

——Religious philosophy. Today's dominant tendencies, characterized by phenomenology, transcendence, and anti-humanism—above all in Protestant circles—are restoring full value to the fundamental givens of the Sunnite *Kalām*. It is understandable if Arab university philosophy has been increasingly imbued with religious philosophy.[1]

——Mysticism and gnosis. It is sufficient to cite the works of Henri Corbin and his chiefly Iranian disciples in order to realize how great a change there has been: what has been taken for more than a century as a confused logomachy (in

1. As with Mohammad Aziz Lahbabi, Yahia Huwaidi, and many others. One should also mention the research of Jacques Waardenbourg, a professor at the University of Utrecht, whose aim is to arrive at a phenomenological understanding of the religious fact through the study of Islam.

Ibn ʿArabī, Suhrawardī, the Ismāʿīlī Duʿāt, Mir Damad, Mulla Sadra, and others, who have been known in the Arab world only indirectly, and through the influence they exerted on al-Afghānī and Muhammad Iqbāl) is once again the expression of an eternal hidden truth that individuals through- out the centuries discover by sudden illumination, in Italy, in Germany, and even in twentieth-century Paris.

——Political philosophy. From the moment that political consciousness, civic consciousness, and historical conscious- ness are no longer regarded as identical; from the moment that one returns from Marx, or even Montesquieu, to Plato (that is, from the positive to the normative); it is then that the whole gamut of Arab political research—which in the nine- teenth century was considered unimportant, whether in its legal phase (Ibn Taimiyya), its philosophical phase (Fārābī), or its individualist phase (Ibn Bāja)—recovers an undeniable up-to-dateness; and one understands how the undertaking of Muhsin Mahdi,[2] and of many others, seems promising.

——Structural history. If history yields its meaning through the inner logic of a structure (at whatever level the latter may be) rather than through the logic of a genetic evolution, then Ibn Khaldūn is actually one of the greatest theoreticians of history. It may well seem tempting to present him as an eminent example of that primacy that can be given to struc- turalist explanation at the expense of historical explanation.[3]

——Formal logic. While serious philosophy is again being reduced to an interminable elucidation of the Aristotelian categories as incarnated and diversified in the propositions of natural languages and the consecutions of mathematical reasoning, it is the innumerable and voluminous commen- taries, and commentaries upon commentaries, which have been relegated to dusty oblivion since the nineteenth-century *Nahda*, that are again attracting the attention of investiga- tors. Why, indeed, should one not exhume subtleties that are

2. Director of the Middle Eastern Center at Harvard and a specialist on Islamic political thought.
3. This is the view of G. Labica in his presentation of the *Muqaddima* (Algiers, 1965).

believed, perhaps mistakenly, to have been discovered in Vienna or Oxford?

——Linguistics, grammar, and rhetoric. No civilization has vested the guarantee of its logico-metaphysical truth in the structures of its language more than the Arab civilization, or in such an unvarying and conscious manner. What Roger Arnaldez has done for Ibn Ḥazm may be generalized for all the great Arab theologians and thinkers of the Middle Ages, and it may be said that all Arabists feel intuitively that they are familiar with at least the rudiments of modern linguistic philosophies (as distinct, of course, from the techniques of linguistic research and presentation).[4]

——Literary criticism. From the moment that one regards as contingent or even denies the distinction between the object of literary creation and the individual subject, and postulates instead a unification of object and subject in a meta-object that is the text—that is in fact language itself (e.g., Roland Barthes' "nouvelle critique")[5]—one finds oneself in the territory of the classical literary criticism that developed from Qurᵓā-nic exegesis. Just as the divine truth incarnates and expresses itself in the materiality of the Qurᵓān, which is the Logos, so do the language and culture of the Arabs express themselves, and nothing but themselves, in poetry or literary prose.

——Poetry. Selecting as examples of modern poetic masterpieces the works of T. S. Eliot, Ezra Pound, and Saint-John Perse, all of whom are exponents of tradition and order, and who take as models and foundations of the "poetic" the attitudes and works of the classicizing periods—that is, periods that in turn take as models reconstructions of presumed classical periods—we will straightaway rediscover a constant of Arab poetry. Is it surprising if the young Arab poets feel themselves in immediate harmony with the attitude of these poets (even if precise and complete understanding is

4. Mohammad Arkoun seemed to be moving in this direction in his public lectures at the University of Rabat (May 1972).
5. Roger Arnaldez, *Grammaire et théologie chez Ibn Hazm de Cordove* (Paris, 1956).

frequently wanting, for this requires familiarity with the details of Greco-Roman, Christian, Byzantine, and Western cultures—a rare accomplishment for a non-Westerner)? The modernity of these poets consists in their recombining of transmitted culture according to a conscious and unvarying code (poetic technique), thus guaranteeing objectivity against universally devalued romantic subjectivity. Now, have all the "modernists" of Arab poetry, from Abū Nuwās to Adonis, done differently?[6]

Finally, let us note that ethnology, psychoanalysis, and economic anthropology, if they cannot be articulated in a direct and clearly demonstrable fashion with the Arab cultural tradition (which is nonetheless a rich vein for prospectors armed with the techniques of these disciplines), all criticize the notion of historical rationality and permit the placing of every society and consequently every culture at an equal distance from a present or an absent God.

It will be asked why I should mention these directions, which together add up to an impressive prejudicial critique of the standpoint I am defending. What, compared with the possibilities offered by these different disciplines, can historicism offer? My intention is to show that the choice of historicism is made not in denial of what contemporary researches have to offer but rather with awareness of what is genuinely attractive but perhaps also misleading about them. I have no wish to deny the Arab intellectual's right to feel a certain comfort and even legitimate pride in the wealth, permanent vitality, and universally applicable value of a culture that is so little supported by socioeconomic structures, even if I must straightaway enter the caveat that these favorable aspects in no way guarantee the future, for they

6. Concerning the last two points (literary criticism and poetics), mention should be made of J. Berque's important remarks in his *Introduction à l'anthologie de la littérature arabe;* also the largely unedited works of Zaghloul Morsy—author of the poem *D'un soleil réticent* that was praised by R. Caillois and R. Barthes—whose "objective" poetry is the result of a minute and methodological reflection on pre-Islamic poetry, Dante, and Mallarmé.

would be equally valid if the Arab people had disappeared five hundred years ago. Furthermore, I have not the slightest intention, by applying a kind of intellectual terrorism, of in any way dissuading young Arabs from participating in these investigations, pending the time when the historical retardation of Arab society shall be made good. Historicism is not presented here as a prerequisite for Arab intellectual achievement, a propaedeutic to all future investigations. Its basic use is to assist in the framing of certain questions that seem to me important, given the present state of Arab society.

To begin with, we are not confronted with a unique circumstance. The very fact that analytical philosophy makes such extensive use of Aristotle, that political philosophy calls upon Plato or Thucydides rather than Machiavelli and Hegel, that modern criticism is restoring to a position of honor the rhetoric of the classical era, itself full of reminders of Latin and Greek rhetoric, that modern poetry makes use of so many Byzantine and postclassical motifs, etc.; all this proves that we are dealing with a general situation that calls specifically for a general judgment. It is evident that the notion of historical retardation has no exact meaning when applied to the cultures of ancient Greece, Byzantium, and the Christian West, or even to classical Europe, but this is solely because it is lost in the notion of historical death.[7] All these cultures can be sources of aesthetic insights, of problematics to be reformulated within a new framework, and of ethical models; in these specific cases, they serve, dead though they are, to exorcise the specter of an end to history as embodied in liberal reason. Consequently, these are willed resuscitations, never spontaneous resurrections. By contrast, if a certain community desired to organize its economy and political regime, its legal order and individual, familial, and social moral codes, its educational system, etc., in the image of one of these cultures, one could then legitimately talk of a

7. This notion is intimately linked with that of totality or systematicity. Cf., concerning this point, the chapter on von Grunebaum (below).

culture retardation, whether this traditionalist point of view was shared by all the community or only by the majority of its intellectual elite. The classical Arab culture might well have been declared finished for good (if, for example, the Ottoman Empire had succeeded from the eighteenth century onward in imposing the Turkish language as the language of everyday use in the Arab provinces, including those provinces it could not conquer, such as Morocco and the northern fringe of the Sahara) and might nevertheless have continued to inspire other men and other cultures, as it did at the end of the European Middle Ages and during a part of the Romantic period, particularly in the Germanic countries. In this situation no one would talk of cultural retardation; I am referring to it precisely because Arab culture is in complete opposition to the other cultures mentioned above, from which only a few isolated and uninfluential groups today claim direct descent. It is desired not merely to draw inspiration from classical Arab culture, but really to revive and reactualize it—if not in the totality of its aspects, then at least in its inner logic. Let it be added that, even at the level at which Arab culture is situated, equivalents exist. According to specialists, as many, if not more, typically modern motifs may be found in the classical Indian and Chinese cultures. In passing, let it also be said that the Indians, whose intellectuals have gone even further in their nationalism and cultural pride than their Arab emulators, have failed to lend plausibility to a single one of their pretensions, whereas the Chinese, who seem to have more titles to glory and until recently were also given to displaying them, are exhibiting an unlooked-for humility in the very hour of their success.

One of the consequences of all this is that the "modernity" that is claimed for the various above-mentioned directions is in fact a "naïve" (in the Hegelian sense) modernity. It is postliberal Western culture that is conceding its modernity to Arab culture, which accepts it as a gift, effortlessly. The Arab intellectual of today who sets out to investigate these directions has, in one way or another, more or less interiorized liberal culture; therefore his sensibility and his intellect have already positively conceded what I call cultural retardation. Yet he does not wish to stay too long in this "apprenticeship," because he sees no profit in it. If he disowns it in so many words, he becomes objectively a cosmopolitan; if on the other hand he remains unconscious of his apprentice's role, he is condemned to be an illustrator. In either event, his researches retain all their practical value. Which does not mean that we cannot appraise them from our own point of view.

This postulated—and conceded—modernity applies only to intellectuals. It is Arab culture that is in question, not society. Even though it would circumspectly be denied that the intellectual is "culturally retarded," it remains to do the same for Arab society, and here we are dealing with a production system that is in competition with others (and not with a theoretical opposition between specific economic rationalities), with a social structure that must at all times prove its viability in the world arena (and not with its inner logic, which is theoretically as total, as elegant, and as plausible as that of any other society whatever), with a practical politics that is in perpetual disequilibrium (and not with elaborate theories about the best form of government), with a language that must constantly prove its creativity and capacity for adaptation in competition with other languages in an accelerating evolutionary situation (and not with a theory of the language at a given moment of its evolution). When one recalls that the rupture between culture and society, between intellectuals and other people, has been one of the constants of our past and perhaps one of the principal reasons for the special evolution of our history, one can regard the modernity of the intellectuals, though far from negligible, as irrelevant. For centuries Italy has had the privilege of providing Europe with "modern" intellectuals and even with visionaries and futurists (labels that are in no sense applicable to the great majority of Arab intellectuals); this fact has not prevented it from prolonging a political, economic, and (in the long run) cultural retardation well into the middle of the twentieth century.

Let me conclude with a remark about postliberal thought in the West itself. Anti-historicist, anti-humanist, anti-rationalist, and anti-subjectivist tendencies are current among the Western intelligentsia—but can the same be said of Western society? What is the immanent vision of the economic organization, internal and external politics, social morality, educational system, and "popular" literature of the West? What rationale underlies the analyses of Western newspapers and the discourses of the "great" at the United Nations and UNESCO? Is it not always that of history as progress, of rationalism in economics, realism in politics, and humanism in literature and the arts? Does the real confrontation take place between societies, in the precincts of the "international" organizations, or between intellectuals in the centers of research? The same is true, moreover, of the socialist East: evolutionism in sociology, realism in politics, populism in literature, etc., have not been transcended any more than has the law of value—this in spite of the experiences of the revolution in its beginnings.

While recognizing the possibilities offered by the reformulation of classical Arab culture in the light of contemporary theoretical trends, while applauding the many efforts being made in this direction, and while feeling as much pride in this culture as any other Arab intellectual, it seems to me important nevertheless to retain the problem of "cultural retardation" at the center of our thinking. Taking this experiential fact as a point of departure—a fact that is daily experienced by millions of Arabs—I shall attempt to describe the logical ties connecting it with historicism and with rationality. I hope to have shown sufficient understanding of viewpoints that are altogether foreign to me to be permitted to present my own point of view in a sometimes trenchant tone.

I

TRADITION AND TRADITIONALIZATION

1 THE ARABS AND HISTORY

The title of this essay echoes that of a book by Constantin Zurayq,[1] *We and History*, which I shall repeatedly cite and sometimes take issue with. First it is necessary to explain the sense in which the author uses the two words.

We refers to both Christian and Muslim Arabs, not only to Muslims: there is a widespread failure to appreciate this fact. Turks, Iranians, Pakistanis, and others have, and have had in the past, notwithstanding their Muslim faith, a view of history that is completely different from that of the Arabs and the analysis of which would call for different premises.

As for the word *History*, it has been customary (for the past century and a half at least and in whatever modern language) to recall that it refers to two quite separate concepts: to history insofar as it is made up of a succession of past events—the objective sum of accomplished facts—and at the same time to the manner of studying these facts and narrating them; that is to say, to the narration itself.

The manifold difficulties that are experienced by the student of history may all derive from this well-known and obvious yet ineluctable semantic duality; for in the last analysis the only historical events are those that occur in and through the act of narration. As a result, we frequently and perhaps increasingly confuse the description that a man makes of events—the logic he imposes upon them if only by way of the succession of words in a sentence—with the objective web of historical facts.[2]

1. Constantin Zurayq, *We and History* (in Arabic) (Beirut, 1959).
2. The novel by J. d'Ormesson, *La gloire de l'Empire* (Paris, 1971), is the best illustration of this necessary distinction. Nothing could more clearly demonstrate that the modern historian does not work on *facts*.

Nevertheless I shall not develop this distinction here, essential and familiar though it is to those who have read any books on methodology, such as those by R. Aron, or H. Butterfield.[3] I shall resort to another distinction, more modest but in my opinion more fruitful: between the study of events (the search for facts, and the techniques of historical description) and the total attitude that a society has toward the aggregate of experienced events; in other words, the place that such a society accords to the past in the pattern of its present and its future and hence of its functioning. It is not a question of a philosophy of history, as with Hegel or Spengler, but of an understanding, an integration of history with collective life. I shall attempt to study these two points of view with regard to Arab society in its classical period and in the modern age and to discern the intellectual and sociopolitical problems that ensue.

I. CLASSICAL ARABIA

How did the classical Arabian society (second to third centuries A.H. / eighth to ninth centuries A.D.) undertake the research and writing of history? Unfortunately no one has made a satisfactory study of this subject.

The studies by Margoliouth and Rosenthal on Muslim historiography, both of which have been translated into Arabic, and the more recent work of Al-Dūrī, remain on a textbook level and do not attempt an analysis of content. In the meantime English-speaking Orientalists have succeeded in establishing some findings that seem reliable.

First, the matter of Arab originality: although attempts have been made to detect foreign influence, whether Greek or Persian (similar attempts have proved successful in the case of Arab philosophy and logic), nothing has come of them; Arab history is not the simple transcription of a word or the

---

3. R. Aron, *Essai sur les limites de l'objectivité historique* (Paris, 1948); H. Butterfield, *Man on His Past: The Study of the History of Historical Scholarship* (Cambridge, 1955).

transposition of a model as with the two aforementioned disciplines. The word *ṭārīkh* is Arabic; the Greek word *historia*, which might have been adopted to convey the same meaning, was also used, but with precisely the opposite meaning of "legend," or "mythical tale" *(usṭūrah,* pl. *asāṭīr)*, in contrast to *ṭārīkh*, which is established, controlled knowledge of past or present facts. It is for this reason that for a long time the Arabs chose to regard themselves as the sole possessors of a true history, other peoples possessing only an accumulation of unverifiable legends.

It therefore seems necessary to regard history, along with grammar *(naḥw)*, as a domain in which the Arabs of the early centuries evinced an unqualified originality.

Why?

In replying to this question, we find ourselves at once at the heart of our problem: history and grammar were sciences that were subordinate to the true science, namely, religious knowledge.

Let us take some examples:

a. Worship. The Qurʾānic revelation unfolded in time, and it was known that certain prophetic sayings had qualified antecedent sayings in the direction either of restriction or of liberalization; it was therefore necessary to know precisely the order in which they were revealed.

b. Private law. When the second caliph, ʿUmar, established a *dīwan*, that is, a list of persons having the right to State pensions (essentially portions of the booty of conquest, payable even to those who had played no active part in the far-flung military expeditions), this list was made according to an order of precedence with graded rates of compensation. The hierarchy corresponded to the order of conversion to the new religion. Thus it was essential to know the history of individual conversions.

c. Public law. The laws of the conquered collectivities, mainly concerned with the regulation of lands and fiscal policy, were largely shaped by the exigencies of conquest. The law varied according as the populations had surrendered without a fight or had resisted before being conquered, and it is easy to see the importance of the conflicting interests involved. For this reason it was necessary to make pains-taking enquiries into the circumstances of the great Muslim conquests, region by region, sometimes right down to the local level.

Even in the early days of the Arab State, this research into priorities was an indispensable undertaking, which grew in importance with the development of the State and subse-quently diversified in accordance with the various aims of historical research.

But we can already discern the outlines of what would later become true historiography.

This historiography had another goal besides that of simple knowledge of the past: the determination of the legal status of individuals and collectivities. Thus it was determined that the first Arab historians were to be for the most part jurists. Since it was concerned with recent events, this historiography was founded essentially on testimony; the first books were *akhbār*, the transmitted accounts of firsthand witnesses. Likewise, historical criticism became essentially an examina-tion of the authenticity of testimonials.

This point deserves to be developed, for much has been written on the subject with the intention of showing that it is the main weakness of Arab historiography.

It must be remembered that recourse to testimony is one, if not the only, foundation of the Muslim religion; for the word of God is transmitted by a witness, the veracious Prophet *(amīn)*. In a sense, it could not be otherwise, for Islam rejects "mute evidence," or miracle; the sole miracle that it accepts, namely the Qurʾān, has the express form of a testimony.[4] Muslims do not conceive of a proof, written or oral, that cannot in the last resort be reduced to the account of a firsthand witness. Moreover, in questions touching so

4. The exegetes have shown that the inimitability of the Qurʾān logically entails a challenge *(taḥaddi)*. Consequently it assumes an evidentiary character.

closely on religion, the principle is adopted that the witness cannot but be sincere, for they are linked to his eternal salvation.

Historiography was motivated by religious faith and sustained by religious faith—a method that is entirely logical if one is always careful to refer it to the original frame of reference.

Thus we are confronted with a mutually sustaining form and content: the narratives relating the life of the Prophet, or the circumstances of such and such an important personage's conversion, or the military expeditions, or anything affecting the interests of those men who were to become the inventors of Arab history, belonged to this specific genre of recital—the *akhbār*, which was set down in writing at a date that has not been precisely determined but was certainly close to the end of the second third of the first century.[5]

This, then, is the first component, a religious one; there exists a second, which one could call the communal political component.

It is known that the Umayyad Empire experienced competitive struggles between the different sectors of Arab society and that the ʿAbbāsid Empire witnessed the development of hostilities which, exacerbated by the religious schisms, had an almost national character.

Gradually effecting integration, the ʿAbbāsid State was to succeed in realizing a modus vivendi among the different groups, above all during and after the reign of al-Mutawakkil. This slow social integration was reflected in the ensuing historiography: to the nucleus formed by the stories of the Prophet were added the titles to glory and antiquity of each of the concerned parties. The pre-Islamic Arabs of the North and South gave their legends (Wahb b. Munabbih, Ibn al-Kalbī, etc.); the Persians gave the long gallery of their Kings of Kings (Ibn al-Muquaffaʿ, al-Dinawārī, etc.); the Rūm gave the annals of Byzantium; and so on.

5. Cf. the article *"Ṭarikh"* (Plessner), *EI* (1) suppl. 231 ff.; R. Blachère, *Histoire de la littérature arabe*, vol. I (Paris, 1951), p. 96 ff.

In these circumstances, the aim of this compilation was to serve the community as such, in accordance with the caliphs' labor of unification, by granting to each group the means of resuscitating the glory of their ancestors—without, however, denying the same satisfaction to the other groups.

So that it could not be used exclusively by any one group, the historical narrative had to be as universal and as neutral as possible; thus it could play a vital role in the formation of that ideology which was gradually to win the allegiance of the majority and which consequently was to be called "orthodoxy" *(sunna)*. The dream of achieving a universal history was realized by Ṭabarī, who, at the end of the ninth century, synthesized all these currents and became the crowned king of historians.

The critical scrutiny of the chain of witnesses continued; but, in the interest of the desired goal of communal unification, a new criterion was added, a new moderation or liberalism in the acceptance of testimonies.

Finally, there is a third component that may be added to the two already mentioned. This, too, is political, but its scope is limited to the interests of a group: the dynasty, the aristocratic family, the legal school, the mystic brotherhood. This historiography of minorities, which was to develop in the shadow of communal historiography, inherited from the latter the same goal and the same method, with, however, certain tangible differences. Such historians were concerned to accumulate titles to pre-eminence in the interest of a particular group bent upon excluding others; in addition to the subtle art of omission, this preoccupation called for the use of a rudimentary rational critique, which in turn called for the elementary data of formal logic.

Why? Because in certain cases there was no longer any guarantee that others would observe the "duty of truthfulness" upon which historical truth depended, particularly when the grave problems that separated Shiʿites and Sunnites were in question. Here, as elsewhere, it was the rupture of the community that opened the way to rational criticism; but often it was reckoned that rational criticism was valid only for others, whereas the first criterion—that of testimonial criticism—would suffice for one's own party. A Shiʿite like Masʿūdī, frequently quoted by Ibn Khaldūn with high approval, made use of rational criticism to ridicule the assertions of the Umayyads, but had recourse solely to the chain of transmission when he dealt with Shīʿism, for in the latter case he was convinced that a follower of the Imām must be constrained by his faith to tell the truth. The necessity for rational critique was increasingly felt in the tenth century, when the idea of a double truth became widespread: one for internal use and the other to be upheld outside the group; the old critical method was no longer sufficient, because it was known that a witness could lie.

But this holds good only for the later periods, never for the initial Prophetic period. In spite of everything, testimony was to remain the foundation.[6]

The Classical Vision of History

Thus Arab society, as it developed during the first three centuries, conferred upon historical narrative a unique form and content. What is the significance of this form and content? In replying to this question we may hope to define the image of narrative history that obtained for the Arabs of the past.

Let us consider, for example, the standard historical narrative, the *Kāmil* of Ibn al-Athīr. First, let it be noted (contrary to the belief of many readers who are misled by the monotonous style) that this work is not homogeneous; three distinct phases may be discerned: a nucleus, consisting of the circumstances of the Prophet's life, is framed by antecedent and subsequent events.

The antecedent history is the sum of narratives concerning each people before the Revelation. The historian's attitude

6. The causes of the fact that historical criticism failed to develop cannot be separated from those of the distinctive trends of the Islamic society and State.

toward this section is peculiar. He naturally makes use of testimonies, but he leaves the responsibility for what is said to the people concerned; without passing judgment, he presents the image that each people would have liked to present. He considers that everything is merely probable and that there is no interest for him in choosing between the different versions. It is even to his advantage to hide nothing, to let the folly and inhumanity of the pre-Islamic world speak for itself. In short, this section is a prehistory, one that is futile and almost without importance.

The kernel is of course the Prophetic period, including revelation, proselytism, conquests, and all the other different chapters, whose names are well known and which receive separate treatment under the titles of *Ṭabaqāt, Maghāzī, Futūhāt*. Here is the narrative's center of gravity, and it is here that there exists perfect harmony between form and content, between method and the logic of the narrative. But one should not believe that this central episode is restricted to the life of the Prophet himself, for on the contrary it was later to serve as a model for the structuring of all the accounts made in self-justification by each and every faction.

The Fātimids and the Almohads are the most convincing examples, but the Zāwiya, and even the families who could pretend to a degree of nobility, were not to understand and construct their past differently, and it is for this reason that the modern historian who utilizes these apologetic accounts must be careful not to confuse a structural stereotype with the real succession of events.

Subsequent history is essentially that of the successors; testimony is still the mainstay, but from a different perspective. If the historian is Sunnite, as is most frequently the case, his criticism of the chains of transmission is much less rigorous. His general attitude is colored by a moderate liberalism; he seeks refuge in the golden mean; he does not accept everything, as he does for the pre-Islamic period (because of its futility), nor is he intractable and sure of his facts, as he is for the Prophetic period (because it is the foundation of all truth); rather, he has an open attitude and accepts everything that may unite the community but rarely anything that could be utilized by one faction against another. Everything is regarded as though it were the prolongation of an epilogue.

This heterogeneous quality explains certain facts that have seemed, and still seem, strange to modern readers. First, the question of the Arab historian's objectivity. Everyone who has studied Arab historiography has acknowledged this objectivity. Von Grunebaum writes in his *Mediaeval Islam:* "Partisanship and courtly flattery notwithstanding, the over-all objectivity of Arab historiography is remarkable;" Margoliouth had previously made similar remarks; but neither of these scholars has brought out the character of this objectivity. In reality, it is identical either with the moral obligation to tell the truth or with the impossibility of knowing the truth: objectivity that stems from a sense of duty or objectivity by default. This means that in the last analysis the true guarantee of an historical narrative (however contradictory this may seem) is the presence of God during the Prophetic period and his absence before and after. The objectivity of the Arab historian has two meanings, both different from the one that would guarantee positivity to the notion of historical truth.

A second characteristic baffles non-Arab readers: the impassiveness of an historian who employs the same style for describing the worst reverses of Arab military history as for describing the heights of gladness. E. F. Gautier, analyzing the instance of Ibn Abī Zarᶜ in *Les Siècles obscurs,*[7] confesses his inability to understand this coldness, doubtless owing to his own passionate approach to knowledge. Natural catastrophes—earthquakes, tidal waves, swarms of locusts—are all recounted with the same wealth of detail as that with which the Arab historian describes official ceremonies, and

7. E. -F. Gautier, *Le Passé de l'Afrique du Nord. Les Siècles obscurs* (Paris, 1937), p. 73. Husain Fawzi makes the same avowal in his *Egyptian Sindbad* (in Arabic) (Cairo, 1962), p. 30.

sometimes even follow immediately after them. One could of
course resort to "good old fatalism" in order to explain this
strange concatenation of elements; but in truth the almost
clinical detachment in question has two meanings, both of
which tally perfectly with those of the previously analyzed
objectivity. During the Prophetic period, reverses are merely
temporary, for the historian is assured of the final result.
During the post-Prophetic period, on the other hand, the
historian adopts a negative attitude toward the facts, for if the
truth is no longer given, no longer guaranteed by a present
God, the difference between success and failure becomes
relative. In the Umayyad period, for example, the conquests
were incontestably successful on this worldly plane, but they
took place under the direction of princes whom the majority
of believers regarded as iniquitous. What was one to think?
The ʿAlids were unquestionably in the right, yet they accumulated setback after setback. Was one to think that successes
denote God's approval and that failures denote his anger? No,
they are mere facts, which must be recorded without further
comment, for they are meaningless.

Subsequently, and in often different political conditions,
the majority of historians remained faithful to this non-
committal attitude; there were few purely official historiographers who were entirely subservient to the needs of their
masters' propaganda, for all retained a somewhat sceptical
distance from what they related.

For this reason the Muslim princes were rarely satisfied
with the histories that were written about them; Aḥmad
Nāsirī was the last to have had bitter personal experience of
this dissatisfaction, with the Alawite Ḥasan I.[8] This is the
more understandable when one recalls that these historians
were for the most part jurists who were not at all sure of the
Qurʾānic legitimacy of the authority under which they lived.

Under these conditions (and thus we approach the close of

8. It seems that the reason for this was the historian's passing of a
favorable judgment on Abd-el-Kader's military talent when he
discussed the latter's brushes with the Moroccan army after 1844.

this first section), what is the status of the historical event for
the Arab historian? It is evident that he does not see events as
positive facts in their own right; they have no self-sufficient
reality.

History, therefore, considered as the totality of these
events, does not constitute a level of reality possessing an
autonomous consistency, where actions can fall into place
and by their very configuration cause other actions to appear.
On the one hand there is a consistency that is of divine
origin: in the Prophet's life, in the beginning of the Almohads,
in the appearance of the Fātimīd Mahdi, and so on—in short,
in every recital conforming to the deeds of the Prophet, and
hence postulating the Divine Presence. On the other hand
positivity is totally lacking; all facts are equal and can appear
in any order whatever. History becomes a domain where
anything is possible (an extremely important observation
when one compares this attitude to others that explicitly
define history as the realm of necessity). In the perspective
of the classical Arab historian, history appears not as a
succession but as a juxtaposition of new beginnings: for an
Almohad the period from the death of the Prophet to the
birth of the Mahdi was not so much one of decadence as one
of inexistence or occultation, during which nothing important
took place. God had withdrawn, and the deeds of men
floundered in futility. The same could be said for the
Fātimīd Shiʿite or the Zaydite.

I have probably frustrated the reader's expectation by
discussing neither philosophical history (Ibn Miskawayh, for
example) nor the philosophy of history (Ibn Khaldūn),
because it does not appear that these two currents can give
us a comprehensive view of a whole society. It is easier to
obtain such a view from the practice of historical narrative
as elaborated and followed by everyone, over and above the
writing of prefaces and forewords. The classical historical
recital should be called neither a "chronicle" nor a set of
"annals," because it is very different from the genres bearing
these names in Asia or in the Christian West; rather, we

should restore to it its distinctive characteristics by bringing its presuppositions to light.

Compared with this past, what is the present situation?

II. THE SITUATION TODAY

As a starting point, let us take a look at Constantin Zurayq's analysis. According to him, contemporary historical practice is characterized by four attitudes:

——First, the traditionalist attitude, which in his judgment remains faithful to the past. He reproaches it for regarding history as being ethnocentric, for having recourse to divine action as an explanation of historical causality, and for failing to adopt a critical stance toward the testimony of great ancestors. He concludes by taxing it with "neo-mediaeval-ism," with reference to similar trends that have appeared recently in Europe.

——Second, the nationalist attitude, be it Arab Unionist or strictly regional (Egyptian, Lebanese, Tunisian, and so on). Zurayq reproaches it for being lost in the past; for having a romantic attitude; for placing history in the service of a political idea, and sometimes quite simply for enslaving it to political power; for overestimating the national past in comparison with that of humanity taken as a whole; for using critical method only when it accords with the nationalist credo of the collectivity and for otherwise disdaining it; and finally for entertaining a confusion between a mystical and a positive explanation of events. In Zurayq's opinion the essential criticism of this attitude lies in the following contra-diction: calling itself nationalist, it denies the very foundation of the modern nation, namely secularity.

——Finally, he cites two other attitudes: the first, Marxist materialist, is of course reproached for its unilateralism in analysis and explanation; the second, positivist, is repre-sented chiefly in modern academic faculties. The author musters all his eloquence to show the desirability—for con-temporary Arab society, that is—of furthering this last move-ment till it becomes dominant.

Similar analyses by Arab intellectuals of the Mashriq or the Maghrib are no longer unusual. Nabih Amīn Faris, another professor at the American University of Beirut, is the author of an article, "The Arabs and Their History,"[9] in which he studies how the manuals of Arab primary and secondary schools are written. He adds to the foregoing reproach another important one that refers to the underestimation of the periods of decadence (for example, the four centuries of Turkish domination, which are nowhere studied), a neglect that falsifies our entire picture of the history of the Arab peoples.

In conclusion, one may say that the present situation is characterized chiefly by the fact that there has been added to the classical vision described above an ideological deformation consequent upon the development of nationalist sentiments, and that the two attitudes mutually reinforce each other in a manner that inhibits the slow diffusion of positivist research methods outside and even within modern academic faculties. History still remains subservient, in contrast to the situation in Turkey, for example, where positivist methods have won the day—at least in the universities.

But is it sufficient to say that? For one could reply: What are the advantages of this "positive" method? The great drawback of Zurayq's book is that, while he admirably describes (like the pure historian he is) his own method, he fails to establish its foundations. He quotes Leopold von Ranke's formula, that the aim of the historian is to describe the event as it really took place; but why, precisely, is this a duty? Why does the description of an event as it really took place have a positive value? After all, did not the classical Arab historian also describe the event exactly as he thought it must have happened, although for different reasons?

He also quotes F. Meinecke—according to whom the greatest revolution that the human mind has known was the historicist revolution—but without explaining the real scope of this assertion. In short, Zurayq's book, which is the work

9. *Middle East Journal* (1954), no. 2, pp. 155-162.

of a scholar and a patriot, will not, despite its undeniable excellences, enjoy the widespread influence it deserves because the author does not undertake to justify his choices on a rational basis.

Let us state immediately that it will not do to say that modern Arab society remains, on the whole, faithful to the vision of history inherited from the past; rather, it finds itself face to face with another society possessing a different vision—a vision to which it is being forced to succumb. The problem, therefore, for Arab society is that it can no longer seek refuge in isolation, that it can no longer remain satisfied with its own vision, still less impose this vision upon others. It is not the intrinsic value of this vision that is at issue, but whether it is adequate to the real relationships obtaining in the world today. The other society is of course industrial society (now represented equally by both East and West). What, exactly, is the vision of history possessed by industrial society?

It is not my intention to do for industrial society what I have done in outline for classical Arab society, or to explain the genesis or trace the development of this vision. I shall confine myself to a few brief remarks.

Behind the praxis of modern historians there exists a certain vision (not necessarily a philosophy) of history—the same vision one suspects is behind certain political actions and the conduct of international relations. It is the vision informing Machiavelli's Phrase, "Time . . . father of all truth," and Hegel's definition, "The historical belongs to us only when we can see the present in general as a consequence of those events in the chain of which the characters or actions described constitute an essential link," or this line of Goethe's, "Tradition, O fool, is indeed a chimera!"

What image can we obtain of this vision? What are its characteristics?

——First, the positivity of history. The event is a fact or an action that determines other facts, other actions; so the present is explained by the past, but the past can be judged by the present. A glorious past that declines into a lamentable present loses, by virtue of this fact, much of its splendor, not only for us but in itself.

——Second, because not all their actions are equivalent, it is possible to pass judgment upon historical participants.

——Third, history is a continuity in which, at each instant, the knowledge of the past informs the present and the present transforms the past, i.e., makes a new picture of the same material.

Objectivity is thus guaranteed by history itself, for even if you do not describe the event as it really happened, you cannot obliterate it, and it revenges itself precisely by informing your present in spite of you; it steals you from yourself, even while you believe that you are master of your own decisions. For the same reason, there is no longer any question of the historian being impassive and detached, for in speaking of others in the past it is always of himself and his own destiny that he really speaks. History and politics meet; historical and civic consciousness are one and the same thing.

Nor is there any question of historical heterogeneity (privileged periods and meaningless, futile periods) or of ethnocentricity (a narrow focus on oneself and a refusal to accept another's opinion of oneself as seen from outside), for the duty of objectivity is unavoidably forced upon everybody as a fact of history. To be sure, ideological deformations are again introduced by a civic consciousness that may well have been led astray, but these deformations are likewise subject to later historical judgment. The historians of the colonial period refused to describe the facts as they really happened; decolonization had demolished their position, and their lucubrations were relegated to the province of self-interested chatter.

This conception of history, which has subsisted in the West since the eighteenth century, if not before, could be described at length. It suffices to take note of the following:

——It has a polar relationship to the conception previously described.

——Just as it has not always prevailed, so also it does not stand as the sole conception of history in the cultural arena of the modern West. There are others, but it is the vision in question that sustains the activity of those at the heart of modern industrial society.

——It is founded, in the last analysis, upon a philosophical a priori. This last point must be recognized if one wishes to escape from the limitations of that unseeing somnambulism which is ignorance of one's own presuppositions. The underlying principle is that God is neither immediately present in the world nor absent, or, in less theological terms, that absolute truth is neither given in advance nor forever denied; for in both cases—truth already conferred or forever lost— history no longer possesses positivity.

In order that history may become the domain of well-defined, serious thought, it is necessary to regard *becoming* as the absolute. When you describe a given fact and wish to give it its true weight, you must not be at all certain of its value or that it possesses an absolute meaning or that it must be forever deprived of such a meaning; rather, you should believe that its meaning will slowly take shape, day after day, event after event, without ever attaining complete realization. All historical action is always in suspense, every sentence is under consideration. This principle is at once the foundation of historicism, democracy, and modern science. The democratic principle means that no one in society possesses political truth, that this truth will only gradually take shape through the procedures of discussion and successive elections —a process that should ideally cause truth to emerge, a truth that the body politic will be able momentarily to agree upon. Similarly, in order that there may be scientific activity, nature must be neither altogether unknowable nor susceptible of immediate knowledge by mystical illumination. This is the foundation of modern historical practice, and it is evident that no one can easily demonstrate—on the level of philosophical presuppositions—the superiority of one vision over the other. It is sufficient for my purpose to make a simple confrontation of the two approaches to history and the two world visions underlying them.

Now, why one and not the other? This is the question we can ask of Constantin Zurayq.

If one wishes to escape from the necessity of justifying history by means of history, one must reply: the only reason is that the society possessing the historicist vision is today dominant. It is the language of historicism that is imposing itself upon the world, and he who would preserve his particular vision is (all things considered) condemning himself to silence.

Analysis shows that Zurayq offers no other reason. This last point allows us to give a few concrete examples in what otherwise might seem an abstract discussion.

Zurayq is manifestly dominated by the Palestinian question, and in the background of everything he writes may be discerned the will to understand one thing: how could the wrong perpetrated on the Arabs of Palestine have been so easily accepted by the entire world? This is why he insists, at the beginning of his book, on the importance of catastrophes in the genesis of historical consciousness. He recalls that failure to understand catastrophes is even deadlier to a people than are the catastrophes themselves.[10] Now in order to understand such catastrophes, their causes must be studied (which entails prior belief in the causal chain of events); the persons responsible must be adjudged (which requires a belief in free will); and, finally, the understanding thus acquired must become the basis for action (which entails prior belief in the possibility of recombining the facts of the past). Therefore effective action calls for acceptance of the modern vision of history and rejection—for the present at least—of the classical vision. To remain faithful, as do the majority of Arabs, to the ancestral vision, and to hope in spite of everything to change the meaning and weight of past events, is to indulge in fatuously wishful thinking.

10. *Op. cit.*, p. 196.

Even here Zurayq unfortunately does not go far enough. In many respects he is justified, for did anyone, over a period of twenty years, discuss the matter of responsibility? That of the Hashemites, for example, or of the prominent Palestinians who collaborated with the English and the Jewish immigrants, or of the Arab states that (it would seem) secretly negotiated from time to time with one or the other. A start has now been made with such accusations, and perhaps not in the best of directions, for one could call attention to the swift passage from the blind faith of one who feels sure of his facts to the sudden despair that has overtaken many of the ruling circles in the Middle East. This passage faithfully reflects the fall from a divinely guaranteed epoch to one that is insensate and accursed—a conception that is a dominant motif, as we have shown, of classical Arab historians.

It is not enough to indicate who is to be held responsible and to stop there; it must be explained why our position on this problem, a position that seems so clear to us, has been accepted by only a minority, and this for merely tactical reasons (as with the Eastern bloc and the neutralist countries), and why our opponents' position, which to us appears so irresponsible, has in spite of everything been accepted by the entire world. It would serve no purpose to cite the role of the fifth columns. In reality, this confrontation of theses is contingent on the larger contradiction between the two visions of history already described. Let us take some examples:

——When we say that in Palestine two historical rights are in opposition, and that logically the most recent and the least discontinuous should triumph, this assertion is not absolutely true, for the Palestinian Jews imbued their past right with a present right, one that was based on cultivation of the land and political action, whereas the Arabs relied essentially upon the theoretical title that is granted by continuous possession. It is true that the Arabs rebelled in 1936; they conducted a heroic struggle, but, abandoned and misunderstood by everyone, they lost hope, and the 1948 war took place virtually without them. It is this fact that was expressed in the speech of the representative of the U.S.S.R. in 1947; this view expressly rejects historical rights and recognizes only the present will of a community, and from this point of view the Palestinian Arabs were not in a strong position. In this clash of policies can be discerned the antagonism between a vision of history that regards legal right as an absolute that is given forever and is inalienable and a vision that regards it as the always revocable consecration of unremitting labor. Twenty years of misery in the camps have done nothing to strengthen the Arabs' position and have by no means provoked others into recognizing their right, which, historical though it is, is vanishing every day further into history. On the other hand, one year of real action has restored a say in the matter to the Palestinians; this is not a political peripeteia, it is a Copernican revolution.

——For fifty years the Arab chiefs have made decisions: Faisal b. Husayn decided to negotiate with Weizmann in 1919, and Abdallah decided to invade the territory of Palestine in 1949. They are, however, by no means willing to acknowledge the *weight* of their actions, the influence these decisions may have on the subsequent development of events. Here is one of the consequences of the ancient vision that denies historical continuity, whereas most people in the modern world think that the responsibility for certain actions must be laid at someone's door: the Russians and Americans expect the Arabs to pay the price for certain actions. In contrast to this attitude of the chiefs, the Palestinians now recognize that they must henceforth accept the consequences of their actions—for which they alone are responsible— whatever these consequences may be. It is precisely for this reason that the world is beginning to listen to them.

——The ancient vision of history implied the possibility of lengthening or shortening the historical development at will. One could let time go by, for one knew that on a certain day

everything would be obliterated and instantaneously reconstructed. Shuquairī's speech, widely publicized by the international press, did not mean that he was going to put the new
inhabitants of his country to the sword, but that they themselves would leave, as if by magic, the land they have
despoiled; in this way will justice be dispensed to the victims,
on that day when the presence of God shall again make itself
felt.

Today the Palestinians in their political declarations show
they have understood that what has been lost by means of a
half-century-old process cannot be regained except by means
of a similar process, which may be equally protracted. To
make and to unmake—to recombine the facts of history—
takes time.

Other examples could be adduced; they would add nothing
to the demonstration. In each instance it has been sufficient to
give an example denoting the influence of the ancient vision
of history and its negative results, and another example
illustrating acceptance of the vision that is now common to
East and West and its positive results.

Thus I hope to have shown why it is essential for the Arabs
(in the present circumstances, and without making a too
hasty judgment about the intrinsic value of the philosophical
principles in question) to adopt one vision of history and to
break with the other—if, that is, they choose to live, for those
in despair are free to choose death.

To a far greater extent than the various struggles for
independence, the problem of Palestine, because of its com-
plexities and objective contradictions, is allowing the Arabs,
while demanding much of them, to become truly conscious of
history. Each one of us must applaud this awakening and see
to it that it does not come to naught; for not only is the Arab's
future at stake, but the interests of other peoples as well.[11]

11. This discussion was written in 1968. Since then the Palestinian
affair has of course evolved, but the problems it sets for the
politico-cultural modernization of Arab society remain fundamentally the same.

2

TRADITION AND TRADITIONALIZATION

I. THE PROBLEM

In sociological literature there is very often a confusion between tradition considered as a social fact and tradition as a system of values, on the ground that it is precisely the latter that characterizes a traditional society. The result is that:

——All sociological analyses of tradition are actually "negative." When one defines tradition as agrarianism, ruralism, passivity, ahistoricity, etc., one is merely translating into negatives the characteristics of "modern" society, that is, of society since the eighteenth century.

——By failing to define the social matrix of tradition, one makes it impossible to determine the focal point for a policy of change; consequently it becomes difficult to imagine anything but an intervention from outside, which in turn implies lack of authenticity and non-participation on the part of the "traditionals."

On the other hand, if one takes care to distinguish tradition as structure from tradition as ideology, one can ask the two following questions:

——Is it logical to impose the problematics of the social sciences, which have developed in the context of a modern society, upon tradition-structure?

——With which social group is it permissible to identify tradition-ideology? This is the question I propose to ask about Morocco.

II. MOROCCO

It has been customary, in order to represent the structure of
Morocco at different periods of its history, to make use of the
geometrical figure of the bisector.

It is said that the power of the precolonial Sultanate was a
sociopolitical bisector between the two components of Moroccan society, namely, the urban population and the tribes,
which were entirely different on all levels—economic, social,
cultural, and religious.

During the Protectorate, the power of the French replaced
that of the sultan and is regarded as having the same role
between the nationalism of the towns and the traditionalism
of the countryside.

Since independence the present royal power is in the same
position between the leftism of the urban parties, labor
unions, and students and the conservatism of the rural
masses.

It is understood (and here there is a vestige of progressive
evolutionary ideology) that in all three periods at least a part
of the urban population were bearers of progress, whereas
the peasantry were preservers of archaism and conservatism
—the hallmarks of tradition. Passing from analysis to the
domain of action, it is easy to see who will be held responsible for backwardness. But when we question history itself,
we find an altogether different image. One of the premises of
the foregoing line of argument is that the precolonial model is
valid for the entire preceding period, since by definition (or
so they say) a traditional society does not conceive change.
But the fact of the matter is quite different.

Political Organization

As it has been described, the power of the *Makhzen* is itself a
novelty; it is the result of a series of very different evolutions,
and it was not until the eighteenth century that the authority
of the *Makhzen* became traditional; that is to say, found its

legitimacy in loyalty to the past. Earlier attempts in this direction had certainly been made, but without success.

The very fact that for the first time eighteenth-century Moroccan society (during the reign of Muḥammad III) either completely or partially accepted fidelity to an alleged model past as sufficient reason for legitimacy, where it had always refused it before, must be explained; it is, in any case, contrary to the definition of tradition as simple fidelity to the past (Max Weber). Hence, one might say that tradition exists only when innovation is accepted under the cloak of fidelity to the past—but then tradition is no longer unquestioning acceptance. Rather, it is a form of acceptance that sets historians many problems.

Culture

I shall set aside folklore, oral traditions, etc., which pose other problems. Confining ourselves to written Arab culture, which in the nineteenth and twentieth centuries was called traditional and was defined by a certain content, mode of transmission, and usage, we can state that these characteristics do not have their origin in the culture itself but in a new situation that developed in the fifteenth and sixteenth centuries. Before this, there had been what one might call a "horizontal" solidarity linking the great cities of the Islamic world with one another rather than with their immediate environs. Thus Fez was intellectually closer to Tunis and the cities of Andalusia than to the villages and countryside by which it was surrounded. Within the framework of this urban culture, the profane, scientific or literary element was dominant—this in spite of what is said in the textbooks. As a result of a change in the economic situation and a weakening of commercial relations, the horizontal solidarity was replaced by a vertical solidarity with the neighboring countryside and mountains.

By reason of this economic crisis, the cultural elite was obliged to transform itself into a teaching body; but because the rural populations that it was necessary to "culturalize" had been isolated for long periods, the urban culture could not be completely assimilated. The sole element of this culture that was entirely valid for the rural society was that which reinforced the community; whence the concentration upon the juridico-social aspect and the decadence of all profane culture.

The content of the tradition that was to develop was the common denominator of an urban elite whose ties with the outside had been severed and a social body that had not taken part in all stages of the Arab cultural evolution. The defining of this tradition was nonetheless to be the work of the elite.

Religious Attitudes

It is customary to contrast the juridico-theological, intellectualist Islam of the towns with the mystico-naturalist Islam of the countryside and to see in the latter a survival of the ancient rural religions. But one must admit that the most intellectualistic profession of faith—that of the Almohads—was the work of highland elements and was rejected by the town dwellers; moreover, the brotherhoods were as much an urban as a rural phenomenon.

The transition from one type of religious attitude to another was linked, as were the above-mentioned cultural changes, to economic change and its social results in the fifteenth century. It was the political necessities of the central authority and the urban elite in an impoverished and dismembered society that accounted for the replacement of a mode of worship based on abstract law by one in which the role of an inspired individual was emphsized. Society was no longer sufficiently united to be guaranteed cohesion and permanence by simple juridical prescriptions. It was necessary to add the direct influence of a visible intermediary, himself linked to other intermediaries past and present, all guarantors of the community's continuity.

Maraboutism is thus by no means the antidote to an urban legalism, but a new religious attitude that a critical situation imposed upon everyone.

What conclusions can be drawn from these briefly summarized facts? Insofar as tradition expresses itself—that is, imposes itself on the community as a model of behavior—the example of Morocco allows us to make the following observations about the formulation of this tradition:

——The conditions: a strong external pressure resulting in economic asphyxia and social dismemberment (the Iberian attacks of the fifteenth and sixteenth centuries).

——The agents: the existing elite with its three components—politico-military, cultural, religious. These three groups are clearly distinguishable in Morocco.

——The intellectual means: those of the preceding period, but pedagogically and dogmatically reformulated in a new educational context.

——The social consequences: a greater cohesion, but in such a framework that this cohesion is in itself a goal and a value; all social life is oriented toward the interior. At all levels, therefore, we observe a process of retrospection.

If one regards tradition as a negation of modernism—as an obstacle to change and progress—it must necessarily be conscious; an unconscious tradition, one that has not been formulated, is opposed to nothing, or else it is a mute, obstinate opposition, which is enacted outside history and may not logically be the object of any "modern" science whatever of politics or sociology.

In these conditions, tradition means traditionalization at the hands of an elite that, finding itself in a position of self-defense, changes its role. It is therefore understandable why this tradition, when it unites the whole of society in opposition to the foreigner, often appears in the guise of an irresistible force and at the same time—from the moment that a definite overture has been made to the elite that formulates and sustains it—also appears very unstable.

One can, if need be, reinforce these conclusions by analysis of two other phenomena of Moroccan history.

1. Nationalism. The nationalist movement in Morocco is all the more difficult to analyze in that it was represented at the time as a reactionary, xenophobic, theocratic move-

ment (because of its loyalty to King Muḥammad V), whereas
the colonial administration, which relied on the brotherhoods, the *shaykhs*, and the great *kaids* of the South,
presented itself as the standard-bearer of modernity. Sociologists, on the other hand, in general define nationalists as
modernists engaged in a life-or-death struggle with their
traditionalist fellow countrymen.

In reality, if one considers the Moroccan society of the
Protectorate in its entirety and the nationalist movement
throughout its extension in time, one sees that there have been
(on all levels: ideology, organization, tactics) two nationalisms: one of denial, turned toward the past and the country's
interior; and another of openness or compromise, playing
the game of colonial rationality. The former was strong in
moments of crisis and was the real driving power behind
independence, while the latter predominated during periods
of dialogue and in the long run was the real beneficiary of
independence.

During the periods of repression (1936-1939, 1951-1955)
there took place a deepening, a traditionalization, of the
nationalist movement; not only were political compromises
rejected, but so also was modern economic organization, and
the past was rehabilitated and social cohesion reinforced. Of
course, we find the reverse of this situation during periods of
negotiation and compromise. In both situations, however,
the same social leadership was involved.

Liberalism, considered as a political philosophy, was not
adopted and developed until the nationalists saw vistas of the
future open before them. Otherwise they preferred the cohesion of their people around a credo descended from the past
to a rupture of their society in the name of an uncertain
future.

2. *Politics after Independence.* The same conclusion can
be drawn from analysis of the policy pursued during the
period 1960-1970, though here the majority of those who
have written on the subject justify this policy with an exact
awareness of the realities of the Moroccan situation.

Also, it is often said that the present regime is a return to that which preceded the Protectorate, precisely because Moroccan society has not evolved sufficiently—this despite the assertions or desires to the contrary of politicians and students who take into consideration only the progress made by the urban population. The policy followed till now would thus be the perfect expression of the Moroccan social structure. There is much naïveté or complacency concealed behind this "objective" analysis.

In the first place, we should note that an essential choice, which has doubtless determined everything else, was made when it was decided not to alter the economic structure. The result is that the administration of *things* continues to be the province of foreigners; for Moroccans, there remains only the government of men—that is, the manipulation of individuals in one direction or another. For this reason, society—and particularly the elite—is once again immersed in an ancient milieu. But it is not tradition that finds expression in this policy; rather, it is the policy that recreates tradition and forces everyone to behave in a traditional way.

The present regime is not a resurgence of a precolonial system, but a continuation of the regime of the Protectorate. Now, this regime of the Protectorate had "read" nineteenth-century Morocco and had derived from it a policy which it endeavored to keep in touch with reality by separating Moroccan society for as long as possible from the new society that colonial capitalism was creating (a dualism at every level). If in fact this continued policy is effective, this is because the new regime has maintained the socioeconomic dualism upon which it was based, and not because it has rediscovered a bogus precolonial substratum.

If there had really been a given tradition which the present regime has merely revealed, one would certainly not have three different formulations of this tradition (that of the nineteenth century, that of nationalism under the Protectorate, and that of the present day) from among which it is still necessary to choose the formulation most faithful to tradition.

If tradition were really a given fundamental that has been rediscovered, we would not find the already mentioned fluctuations of nationalism. Tradition is all the more affirmed as the future prospects are dark.

In reality when we trace this movement of reaffirmation, resurrection, or rehabilitation of tradition, after an interlude during which triumphant nationalism forgets its traditionalist vocation, and when we relate it to different developments on the economic, social, and cultural levels, we cannot help noticing that the same groups are playing the same roles today that they played in the past: a politico-mililtary elite *(Makhzen)*, an economic elite (the urban middle class), and a cultural elite (the urban petite bourgeoisie). In a new situation and with new means we again find, however, the same conditions of economic pressure from outside, the same failure on the part of these elites, and the same phenomenon of readaptation, of return toward the self, toward the interior, toward the past. A new tradition answers to a new situation; everything is reformulated and reinterpreted. But essentially the elite prefers, to outer- and future-directed activity—which is always problematic—an activity directed toward the past, the goal and results of which, in terms of political and economic power, are assured. Let us note also that those who wish to find themselves in the mirror of tradition never play an active role in this movement.

From this brief discussion, we can conclude:

——Tradition, in order that it may be established and survive, demands as much activity as "progress," but in a different direction. The notion of an eternal tradition maintaining itself by itself is an illusion, a misleading extrapolation from liberalism's negative definitions.

——The maintenance of a tradition is the work of a politico-cultural elite whose activity, which may seem deviant to others, brings them as many satisfactions as would action of a modernist orientation.

——To say that the strength of tradition lies in inertia seems a mere play on words, for formulated tradition does not express the reality of those who are represented as traditionalists, and it can claim no strong adherence from them; its strength is derived from the lack, in the eyes of the elite, of a concrete alternative. The elite therefore continues to act in a way calculated to ensure the continuance of its role.

From the moment that an alternative appears on the horizon, tradition is no longer supported by anyone, and its intrinsic weakness stands revealed. (Owing to the fact that the central power is sometimes incapable of fulfilling all its promises, the case of a tradition's survival after a period of accelerated modernization is very different and poses special problems.)

III. METHODOLOGICAL CONCLUSIONS

If the examples taken from Moroccan history are not too exceptional, and if it is possible to find at least analogous circumstances in the vast world of Islam, then the following remarks may be advanced as discussion points:

1. Where there is adequation between tradition as structure and tradition as value, and where there is a homogeneous society (two presuppositions that are nearly always taken for granted by sociologists), we are assuredly dealing with societies that deny history, and the utilization of such instances in the construction of sociological models designed for general application is necessarily ideological. The comparisons are mere illustrations, and the definitions arrived at are so abstract that the conclusions are for the most part given in the premises.

2. In the numerous cases where there is a formulated tradition, when the lived tradition may therefore be distinguished from tradition as value, it is the latter that may be directly studied.

In these circumstances we are confronted with organized, evolving societies; here the questions of the social sciences are legitimate. Tradition will appear above all in the guise of a traditionalization effected by an elite at different stages of its history. Tradition *qua* structure is always inferred as the theoretic basis of what is formulated. A rigorous, well-founded analysis of this mode of tradition has nowhere been undertaken; the ostensible studies to be found in the works of sociologists are merely reverse images of modern industrial society. In reality when we take care to adopt the perspective of each of these so-called traditional societies, and when we follow their historical developments, we realize that each society has also a residual structure that may be called tradition, just as the entire group of these societies is defined as traditional by those who adopt the perspective of the industrial West.

3. The notions of passivity, inertia, stasis, homogeneity, etc., with which these societies are described are the consequences of this negative, residual comprehension; they are the result of a method, not descriptions of a directly grasped reality. The result is that the voluntary and ideological aspect is denied, as are the differences of attitude toward the formulated tradition within the traditional society itself. The pseudo-sociological connection that is emphasized between traditionalism and rural folkways or tribalism is likewise a methodological *a priori*. Once a dynamic viewpoint is adopted, both tradition and innovation, or traditionalism and progressivism, are seen as the achievement of an elite— nearly always urban—that acts in one direction or the other according to the circumstances in which it finds itself.

4. The clarification of these circumstances gives rise to the question of the elite's freedom of choice. Sociologists deny this freedom in principle: their negative definition leads them to state that tradition is a destiny, that progress is necessarily an intervention from outside. One can, as a matter of fact, say exactly the opposite: tradition is choice made in response to foreign intervention. Not to see this is to deny the realities of hegemony. The traditionalization of a society is often, perhaps always, contemporaneous with a threat of hegemony

from without; it can neither be the cause of such a threat nor the excuse for it.

5. This analysis introduces an element of dialectical evolution. In a traditional society the obstacle to progress is not entirely internal; rather, it is a resultant, composed of an outside influence, always manifested as a threat, and a reaction peculiar to the society in question. If the outside pressure persists or intensifies, traditionalization also intensifies. That is why all the static models proposed by the sociologists—models that do not take account of this factor of outside pressure—must show tradition as an insurmountable obstacle and by that very fact must consolidate it; for such models nourish the scepticism of the elite about its own future in a world already dominated by others. The sole antidote to tradition is hope, the vision of an unobstructed future; this is the profound meaning of revolution, under whatever label.

This analysis permits us to understand the inverse situation: that of a rapid evolution—a phenomenon that never fails to astonish sociologists. The static models used, which give undue weight to tradition, make all evolutions incomprehensible. But if tradition is an elitist ideology for periods of contracted vision, it will be readily understood that at the first clearing of the horizon the elite again takes its place in history, that is, changes the direction of its activity.[1]

1. The works whose conclusions are implicitly criticized in this chapter are primarily the following: David E. Apter, *The Politics of Modernization* (Chicago, 1965); Douglas Ashford, *Political Change in Morocco* (Princeton, 1961); D. Lerner, *The Passing of Traditional Society* (New York, 1958).

3

THE ARABS AND CULTURAL ANTHROPOLOGY: NOTES ON THE METHOD OF GUSTAVE VON GRUNEBAUM

I

It is certainly not easy to decide if it is in the interests of Muslims, and of the Arabs especially, to take the works of Orientalists as a starting point for an analysis of their culture. (An Orientalist is defined as a foreigner—in this case, a Westerner—who takes Islam as the subject of his research.)

The disadvantages are almost immediately apparent: we find in the Orientalists' works an ideological (in the crudest sense of the word) critique of Islamic culture. The result of great intellectual efforts is for the most part valueless. Western Orientalism is not Western "science" applied to a particular subject. Compared with other disciplines, it makes use of a limited range of methods—a fact which may be imputed to a variety of causes (curricula of study in Western universities, choice of personnel, objectives pursued, etc.). The caste of Orientalists constitutes part of the bureaucracy and, for this reason, suffers from limitations that badly inhibit the free creation of new approaches or even the application of those that already exist.[1] As a result the criticism of Orientalism by Muslims almost never succeeds in isolating the methodological foundations of the various points of view, in order to reject them, adopt them, or utilize them

1. C. Wright Mills' observations on sociologists in general (in *The Sociological Imagination* (New York, 1959), ch. 5) are applicable to Orientalists as a specific group.

for other ends; rather, it deals with specific analyses, judgments, and descriptions in order to relate them directly either to the great political disputes that today separate the West from Islam or to the religious controversies of the past. It therefore adopts by implication the restrictive epistemology (which has often failed to keep up with the overall evolution of Western science) of superficially examined texts. Just as the Orientalists are independent both of the church and of the modern universities, so also their Muslim critics, whether modernists or apologists, form a special caste that is identical neither with the class of ʿulamā nor still less with the intelligentsia of the Muslim countries.

There is, however, an advantage to be derived from a critical examination—at a certain level—of the Orientalists' labors. It resides in the fact that this examination must inevitably lead toward a new form of the munāzara (dialectical controversy), toward a realization of the requisite conditions for the establishment of a universally valid truth. Without embarking on a lengthy discussion of the existence or nonexistence of such a truth, I will nonetheless state that there can be only two possibilities in this domain: the definition of this truth or an endless diversification of points of view. It is, of course, easy to isolate non-Muslim Orientalists with imperialistic designs. But what is one to make of those trained in Eastern Europe, China, Japan, and Latin America, whose international stature grows from year to year? Within Islam itself, how is one to reconcile the point of view of the Shiʿite with that of the non-Shiʿite, or the Turkish view of Arab Islam with the Arab view of the Ottoman Caliphate? Again, within the Arab camp the same cultural fact can be, and already is, subject to diverging evaluations.[2] If we have no desire for the fragmentation of research to result in a

2. As examples of these different viewpoints, let me cite the following: Fazlu Rahman, *Islam* (London, 1966); Henri Corbin, *Histoire de la philosophie islamique* (Paris, 1964); Homa Pakdaman, *Al-Afghani* (Paris, 1966); Nur al-Din Zeine, on Turko-Arab relations; Anis Syaigh, *Al-Hāshimiyun* (1966); and Moh. Ghazzali, *Haqiqat al-qawmiyya al-ʿarabiyya* (1969).

cultural protectionism where each keeps his patrimony for himself and forbids others to touch it, we must submit to new rules of the *munāzara*.

II

The framework of the critique having been determined, why have I chosen Gustave von Grunebaum? Primarily because he stands at the crossroads of several Orientalist traditions. Brought up in Vienna, he is heir to the German philological and historicist tradition that was a redoubtable adversary of the Muslim reformists. Thanks to the cosmopolitan tradition of the Austrian capital, he was also in a position to benefit from the other schools of European thought: French, English, Italian, Russian. Emigrating to the United States, he joined the University of Chicago, which is very much under the sway of German sociology and functions in this field as the training center for teaching personnel of other universities. Chicago is known for its research in the domains of epistemology, the methodology of the social sciences, anthropology, the sociology of religion; that is, in all the areas in which the Germans of the Wilhelmine period excelled. In this milieu von Grunebaum, the philologist and specialist in classical poetry, transformed himself into an anthropologist of Islam. As so often happens in the United States, von Grunebaum was soon given a responsible position; accordingly he left Chicago to direct the Center for Near Eastern Studies in Los Angeles, where he was encouraged to apply his general characterizations of Islam to the modern world. Undergoing the influence of the political sciences in this new milieu, he nevertheless maintains a certain independence of method that I shall have occasion to emphasize.

The exemplary quality of von Grunebaum's work, as far as creativity is concerned, derives from the diversity of elements that nourish it: a sound classical education, plus a good knowledge of Byzantium; familiarity with the principal languages of Islam (Arabic, Persian, Turkish); and a diversity of methodological approaches—philology, cultural sociology, anthropology, the political sciences. Moreover, moving as he did from a German to an American environment, and aware of what was happening in other domains (Slavic, Chinese, Latin American studies), von Grunebaum was very conscious of the necessity to redefine the methods of academic Islamic studies.

Because of this exemplary quality—I refer to the creativity of his achievement, not to the results—it is useless to confine oneself to a superficial criticism of his works by concentrating merely on his individual or group prejudices; it is necessary to go straight to the roots of his vision, to his challenge to Islam. Although he sympathizes with many aspects of Islamic life, and sees in the type of the traditional Muslim a perfect personification of a certain antihumanist humanism, he never indulges in insincere flattery. As time passes, and as the material and political renaissance of Islam unfolds, so do von Grunebaum's judgments become increasingly negative and his challenge more conspicuous. One can with good reason prefer this attitude to one concealing other than disinterested motives.

III

Attempting to determine our author's methodological postulates, we find that at a certain level he is very conscious of his presuppositions, but that at a deeper level he is far from being explicit, doubtless in the belief that certain definitions are self-evident. It is our task to examine these implicit assumptions.[3]

3. This is not an exhaustive study of von Grunebaum's work. I have used the following studies: *Islam: Essays in the Nature and Growth of a Cultural Tradition* ((London, 1955) (referred to below as *Isl.*); *Medieval Islam: A Study in Cultural Orientation* (Chicago, 1946) (referred to as *Med. Isl.*); *Modern Islam: The Search for Cultural Identity* (New York, 1964) (referred to as *Mod. Isl.*); "Islamic Literature, Arabic," *Near Eastern Culture and Society*, ed. T. Cuyler Young, pp. 48-65; *"Le Problème des échanges culturels,"*

From the beginning, in his studies of poetry, he declines to conceive of classical Arabic poetry either as a simple object of aesthetic pleasure or as a simple source of historical information. He rejects both the idea of an immediate communicability and the idea of an absolute incommensurability between the Arab and European sensibilities. He prefers to take this poetry as the expression of a fundamental modality of the spirit, that of Islamic civilization as a whole. He himself relates this perspective to what he calls the neo-humanism of the period between the wars. We know from elsewhere that it has a more distant origin and that it is found at the intersection of neo-Kantianism and Hegelian historicism—the birthplace of most of the influential schools of thought in the domain of the social sciences. It is revealing that von Grunebaum began his studies with poetry, for this is the only field in which he has carried out concrete, specific research; later he proceeds to general theory and remains there. It is easy to appreciate that the very special characteristics of Arabic poetry have profoundly influenced his thinking. The transition to "culturalism" is then easier to understand. For cultural anthropology, as represented by A. L. Kroeber, is inspired by German thought, and in America von Grunebaum has returned, as it were, to his sources. As time went on, he was to clarify his method, but all the essentials had already been laid down in his studies of Arab aesthetics.[4] What are the fundamental notions of this method?

Etudes dédiées à Lévi-Provençal, vol. I (Paris, 1962), pp. 141-151; Islam: Experience of the Holy and Concept of Man (Los Angeles, 1965) (referred to as Exp. Hol.); "The Sources of Islamic Civilization," Der Islam (Berlin, March 1970), pp. 1-54; "Le Rêve dans l'Islam classique," Le Rêve dans les sociétés humaines, ed. von Grunebaum and R. Caillois (Paris, 1963); "La Convergence des traditions culturelles en Méditerranée," Diogène (1970), no. 71, pp. 3-21.

4. See primarily "An Analysis of Islamic Civilization and Cultural Anthropology," Mod. Isl., pp. 40-97.

1. The first and in fact the only basic conception is that of culture, which serves to delimit the very object of study. I shall not attempt to analyze here the content of this notion, for that would properly entail an historical account and critique of the whole field of German-American cultural anthropology. It is sufficient to note that von Grunebaum takes it in the form elaborated by Kroeber after it had been disencumbered of all the mystico-romantic implications it had retained for Dilthey and the neo-Hegelians.[5] The notion of culture is severed from its origin in the concept of objective spirit, which for Hegel was a stage in the evolution of Spirit. It remains only to define an epistemological object, and an autonomous science of culture will have been made possible, taking its rightful place beside the other sciences: history, the philosophy of history, sociology, political economy. It is immediately apparent that serious problems arise precisely when it is a question of demarcating culture from other objects of study: society, civilization, ideology, morality, art. Von Grunebaum, following the authority of Kroeber, puts aside (in his writings at least) the problematic aspect of this science of culture, though the results of his particular analyses remain, in the end, problematical.

The delimitation in question is made possible by the postulation of an invariant, which acts not so much as a determinant as a unitive principle,[6] or rather as a principle of

---

5. Nevertheless some of these implications remain, as the following sentences from *Med. Isl.* (pp. 62-63) attest: "Early in the Middle Ages the Latin West had come to accept the idea that civilization flows from East to West. . . . Europe vaguely realized it had no longer anything essential to learn from its age-old opponent (Islam)."

6. This idea was vulgarized by Ruth Benedict in particular, in her *Patterns of Culture* (New York, 1934), chs. 2 and 3. Cf. the Foreword to *Isl.* by Robert Redfield and Milton Singer, in which the principal ideas are traced to their origin in the work of A. L. Kroeber. Here we read that "in this sense total culture patterns are more readily established for some complex cultures—the sacred book civilizations —than they can be for the simpler primitive cultures where they remain implicit and 'unconscious canons of choice.' " Cf. also *Med. Isl.*, p. 320; *Isl.*, p. 243; *Mod. Isl.*, pp. 53, 80.

exclusion.[7] Von Grunebaum makes use of this notion many times in his studies of cultural exchange, influence, and evolution. Influence and exchange take place under the control of this invariant, whereas evolution is the accumulated resultant of those choices that point in the same direction.[8] Culture is therefore conceived essentially as a principle of exclusion, and the period in which the characteristic cultural direction first takes shape or clearly appears—a direction that will be manifested in all the successive choices —is the matrix of the culture in question. This matrix is neither objectively nor subjectively revealed (i.e., revealed neither to the society itself nor to the investigator) until the end of the historic process. It is at the outset (of both the historical process and the researcher's investigation) a simple hypothesis, an objective and subjective probability, which is verified only in and through history. As it finally appears, culture is an aggregate of values structured around a principle of choice and exclusion—an aspiration.

We can already foresee the problems arising from this postulation of a unitary principle as the fundamental "datum" that history alone reveals.

2. The consequence of the above postulate (and a means of verifying it) is that culture constitutes a closed system, since the principle of exclusion operates at all levels. If attempts to systematize a given culture around a structuring principle fail, it is either because the culture in question is not in fact a culture in the real sense, or because the required principle eludes investigation owing to its subtlety. But in the framework of cultural anthropology, a rejection of the very notion of system cannot be envisaged.

Let me say here that this notion of system is an imprecise

7. "Every motif chosen by Islam meant a motif rejected." *(Exp. Hol.*, p. 6.)

8. "In this synthesis of the disparate the *Arabian Nights* present a likeness on a small scale of Islamic civilization as a whole. . . . Islamic civilization is thoroughly syncretistic, and it proves its vitality by coating each and every borrowing with its own inimitable patina." *(Med. Isl.*, p. 319.)

one, seeing that all schools of the social sciences make free use of it, and everything hangs on what is the actual basis of the idea. Following Kroeber, von Grunebaum uses it in the sense of a recurring pattern, a similar solution given in different domains to problems that are similar in form (e.g., atomism in poetry, in natural philosophy, in political science). Once a principle of integration and exclusion is postulated at the heart of culture, its consequences appear as extremely dissimilar social facts—moral, aesthetic, political, ecological, etc.—which can nonetheless be reduced to so many significations directly mirrored in this principle. Thus "system" essentially forms the plane of heavenly existence—that is, of meaning—to which the sociohistorical facts of a given culture are gradually reduced, both within the objective scheme of history and within the mind of the historian. This system, or this existential plane, remains always ideal, since the investigator will not succeed in making it mirror all the facts with which history provides him; but whenever he does succeed in connecting such and such a fact to the first principle, thus conferring significance upon it, he inscribes it in the heaven of Ideas, which, originally empty, is gradually filled with stars. It will be seen that "system," so regarded, is a distant metamorphosis of the Hegelian totality, but one that has been reduced to an immutable content of the philosopher's Knowledge and that has accordingly lost its intrinsic necessity. Here it constitutes one possibility among numerous others that keep its company in history, which is only the spatialized domain of the human mind.

If we do not make a precise definition of the content, as it appears in the results of his analysis, of this notion of system, we run the risk of confusing it with other notions bearing a formal resemblance to it, such as structure, model, totality, aggregate, or field—the more so as practically all the social sciences operate with two notions: one that confers unity upon the object of study, and another that introduces a principle of evolution. It is the express task of criticism to surmount these formal resemblances.

3. The result of all this is a significant reduction of every social fact. At all levels of reality, the historian is concerned to identify actual reproductions of—rather than correspondences to—the process of elimination, hence realization, of the first principle. The total evolution of theology—that is, the process by which all the notions used therein come to belong to the same semantic level—has to be reproduced in the evolution of the society and the State, public morality and the formation of ideal human types, literary expression and urban structure, etc. In the long run, the same essential pattern of the culture in question must be reproduced in space by the city, in words by the written work, in time by politics, and in eternity by theology. All systems of relations must, therefore, be capable of being neatly folded one on top of another, being in fact isomorphic.

The big problem will be to justify, in its turn, this reduction. In order that it may not seem to be of the analyst's fanciful choosing, one must ascribe it to the historical unfolding itself. The historian has only to rediscover the historical movement. The origin of this conception is plainly Hegelian, but it is here deprived of its Hegelian justification and made over as that which grants the very possibility of existence to an autonomous science.

IV

Armed with these presuppositions, von Grunebaum launches into the study of Islam. It is evident therefore that any judgment of his results should include an evaluation of the presuppositions adumbrated in the foregoing pages. Furthermore, all those affirmations (and they are many), which may denote a fundamental antipathy on the part of the author, should be ignored. [9]

9. "Islam is eminently human in that it takes man for what he is, but it is not humanist in that it is not interested in the richest possible unfolding and evolving of man's potentialities." (*Med. Isl.*, p. 230.) "Arrested in its growth during the eleventh century, [Islam] has

From the outset, von Grunebaum devotes himself to Islam as *culture;* this is the important point to be noted and discussed. The concept of culture is, to repeat, problematic; yet this unknown entity of Islam, whose spirit, unitary principle, or aspiration is to be described, is at the outset identified as a culture. The historian's entire undertaking will be burdened with this initial imprecision.

This postulated spirit, this vital essence of Islam, cannot be directly apprehended. It can be disclosed only by an attempt (in theory many times renewed) to find again the inner logic of Islam's history. The only available means is that of a two-way comparative process, one phase of which centers on similarities and agreements between different domains within Islam, while the other centers on differences and contrasts without. The analysis always has four variables:[10]

Similarities	*Contrasts*
the Muslim city	the classical city
| |	| |
the Islamic Umma	the Greek polis

When the author undertakes to analyze his material and goes beyond mere summary, there is a continual play of such intra- and intercomparisons. It is by this sole process of successive accommodations—direct or mediatized identifications—that he arrives at a determination and an understanding of a given fact. For this reason, which pertains to method, his propositions amount to so many value judgments.

1. Intracomparison. Von Grunebaum's program of studies, long or short, is nearly always the same: a theory of God that is succeeded by a type of piety, itself succeeded by a political theory—this is the fundamental sequence, the "matrix of

---

remained an unfulfilled promise . . . the relative backwardness of Islam was never quite to be eliminated." *(Ibid.,* pp. 322-323.) "Islam can hardly be called creative in the sense that the Greeks were creative in the fifth and fourth centuries B.C. or the Western world since the Renaissance." *(Ibid.,* p. 324.)

10. Cf. "The Structure of the Muslim Town," *Isl.,* pp. 141-155. "For the unity of the Muslim town is functional, not civic." *(Ibid.,* p. 147.)

Islam." Why? The theory of God arises from a textual reading
that is verified positively by individual experience and verified negatively by the destiny of the Muslim community.
It is with this matrix as a touchstone that subsequent developments in various areas are evaluated: theology, *fiqh* (polity, urban law, social structure), personality types (biographies, historiography), types of stylization (poetry, *adab*).
This procedure is logically divided into two phases. In the
first phase, factual history is made ample use of,[11] and it is
easy to see why. If all known facts were directly combined,
Islam would be dismembered as an historically given unit and
would be reduced to the theoretical structure of possible
societies. We would thus be left with a sort of functionalism
applied to the past. In order to escape from this, it is required
of history to give the initial canvas; that is, to establish the
meaning and direction of the structuring principle. This is
what separates the "culturalism" that is applied to "primitive"
societies from that of von Grunebaum, who is grappling with
an eminently scriptural society. It remains for us to see if this
precaution is sufficient to ward off subjectivism.

2. Intercomparison. Here, also, two levels can be distinguished. The Christian West and Byzantium are contrasted
with Islam but share the same historicity, the differences
between the three units being of a linear order. The modern
West is contrasted with the three ensembles, in increasingly
extended perspectives:

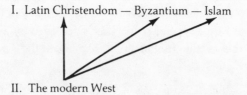

I. Latin Christendom — Byzantium — Islam

II. The modern West

Naturally, von Grunebaum regards the paradigms as already known and takes his material from wherever he can. As
every identification of Islam will depend on that of the

11. Above all, in the chapters "The Mood of the Times," *Med. Isl.*,
and "The Profile of Muslim Civilization," *Isl.*

reference cultures, we shall inevitably find that, to the degree that the three protagonists of the medieval world are individualized, incertitude will prevail about their common origin (which is ancient culture) and above all about the reference culture par excellence (which is the modern West). The ancient world, too, seems to be conceived as a sequence in which Greece forms the classical period and Rome the period of decadence. This ancient world nourishes alike both Islam and Byzantium, which together constitute an almost unique case of cultural parallelism,[12] whereas the relation between the classical world and the medieval Christian West remains obscure.

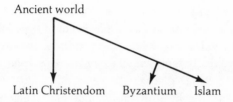

Ancient world

Latin Christendom   Byzantium   Islam

The two procedures can be represented thus:

I

		God	Man	Society	Expression	Science
	MATRIX	Qurʾān	Piety	Sects	Poetry	
ISLAM		Theology	Heroic types	*Fiqh*	*Adab*	
		Mysticism	Types of stylization	Ecology (city)	Architecture Decoration	

12. In his contributions to *The Cambridge Medieval History* and elsewhere, von Grunebaum has studied the parallel developments of feudal agrarian structures in Byzantium and in the ʿAbbāsid Caliphate, as well as similarities between forms of piety, structures of artistic expression, etc. It is a question not of mutual influence but of a flowering of the same basic concepts. Cf. *Med. Isl.*, p. 30.

II

	Classical world	Byzantium	Latin Christendom	Modern West	Islam
God					+ +
Man					—
Society-State					—
Expression					X
Science					—

This diagram is of course theoretical; it is not filled out completely, since it is above all a matter of filling in the spaces of a single column. If von Grunebaum's definitions are considered value judgments, the results of his investigation can be effectively represented in the above manner, taking as basis the cultural matrix: the Qurʾānic Logos, manifested positively in the lives of individuals and manifested negatively in the struggles of sects.

Naturally, this is only a schematic compression of an investigation that in theory ought to have followed a very roundabout path. The unitary principle should not have been isolated (this is a requirement of clear and rational exposition) unless numerous unproductive tries had first been made. The starting point is immaterial provided that one proceeds by means of dualities: historiography and theology, for example, or poetry and forms of morality, prose and architecture, polity and heroic types, etc.; then, by successive rapprochements and differential reductions, we should eventually succeed in embracing at a glance the parallel sections of the various concrete manifestations of the spirit of Islam. We have no means, to be sure, of checking if the actual research was equal to the demands of this exacting method. The danger of subjectivism attends every step of the investigation, and in the final analysis the value of the results are proportional to one's estimate of the method.

V

Before embarking on a critical appreciation of von Grunebaum's results, it is well to clarify certain conclusions that
inevitably proceed from the method itself.

1. Inasmuch as the fundamental aspiration is a principle of
integration and, above all, of exclusion, all the manifestations
of a culture will not be a priori possible, or (more exactly)
probable. When it is a concealed aspect of a culture that is
being studied, or an aspect that historically came to nothing,
an investigator who is outside the culturalist perspective must
necessarily run the risk of pursuing spurious explanations.
For the culturalist, therefore, there are questions that should
not be asked and researches that should not be undertaken
unless there is the intention of placing in *a contrario* relief
that original choice which has explicitly condemned all such
enquiry to pointlessness. The selfsame impulse that allows us
to isolate the matrix of Islam will allow us to delimit its areas
of manifestation at every level. Individual experiments, frag-
mentary contributions or borrowings, short-lived but widespread enthusiasms—all can at one time or another be
identified; but sooner or later they are neglected, forgotten,
eliminated, or condemned, according to their importance and
according as they threaten the integrity of the society's
essential aspiration.

Now, it is immediately obvious that this attitude will
influence the direction the investigation takes and the evaluation of the results. It follows from this attitude that neither
urban law, nor tragedy, nor dramatic poem, nor theory of
State, nor plastic art can really exist in Islam.[13] Admittedly,

13. Concerning urban law, von Grunebaum minimizes the researches
of R. Brunschwig on Muslim jurisprudence and the medieval town:
"The pragmatic nature of much of Muslim jurisprudence is as clearly
discernible as its reluctance to set up special areas of jurisdiction."
(*Isl.*, p. 154.) As for drama: "If Sunnite Islam has failed to develop
a drama, acquainted though it could have been with the Indian
tradition, this is due not so much to historical accident but to a
concept of man for which the peculiar conflict of tragedy could not
arise." (*Exp. Hol.*, p. 12.) This idea was taken up by Moh. Aziza in

the analyst will not be a priori discouraged from his research,
for the reason that the matrix is revealed only by successive
approximations; trials are requisite at every step of the
investigation and in every domain; the undertaking is theoretically endless and it is just as important to consider what was
excluded as what was actually realized. Nonetheless, it is
impossible to deny the negative character of many of von
Grunebaum's judgments on those beginnings (of urban law,
autobiography, and scientific methodology) that have come
to light; these in fact present him with serious problems. If it
turns out that there have been numerous adventurous trials
and experiments, what becomes of the integrative power of
the fundamental *principle?* Von Grunebaum exhibits a
healthy reaction against the superficial and peremptory opinion that would attribute absence of development to racial
incapacity. (One has only to recall what has been said on the
subject of the Arabs' lack of imagination, civic sense, historicity, and scientific bent.) He shows here a moderation of
judgment that is, however, only the reverse side of that
narrowness of scope he initially concedes to Islam.

2. The search for the fundamental aspiration, or matrix, of
Islam is necessarily the description of a classicism and a
tradition: the three notions amount to the same thing. At the
beginning of the process the matrix is postulated as a simple
possibility of reorganization of the range of meanings available to a given culture—a possibility that is realized only in
time. The integration and exclusion of ideas, institutions, and
objects so that a system of values shall be achieved does not
happen automatically but is the work of men organized into
groups. The matrix does not emerge as an objective reality
until it is firmly settled in a group's mentality, at which point

---

his *Islam and the Theatre.* As for the State: "The early history of
Christianity and [the] dichotomy of Christian government preserved
the West from the organizational breakdown that resulted from the
unrealizable expectation which Islam had to place in the state."
(Isl., p. 135.)

a tradition is formed; it is not an objective structure present at all times but an achievement of the men who manifest it in the full light of actual history. Thus the notion of an unconscious classicism is, from this point of view, useless, even unthinkable; classicism is said really to exist only when it is reconstructed by a tradition in the pattern of a presumed past—an attempt that follows an awakening to the reality of decadence. Isomorphism between outward expression and matrix exists only from the moment when a given culture tries (without success) to perpetuate an equilibrium that appears as such only after it has been irremediably lost.[14] It is after the eleventh century (the great defeat of the first Crusades) that Islam finds its matrix, whereas the preceding period (of the ninth and tenth centuries), which the historian regards as the apogee, cannot be the central period for the cultural anthropologist precisely because of the lack of definite contours; nothing in this period has been finally incorporated or finally rejected. In this sense the adjectives von Grunebaum couples with the word "Islam" (medieval, classical, modern) are neutral or even superfluous: there is no difference between classical Islam and medieval Islam or simply Islam. A quick perusal of the three books will convince the reader of the truth of this assertion. As for modern Islam, this, as we shall see, is problematic—as the subtitle of the book that deals with it clearly indicates: *The Search for Cultural Identity*. There is, then, only one Islam: an Islam that mutates within itself when tradition takes shape on the basis of a reconstructed "classical" period. From that time onward the actual succession of facts becomes illusory; examples can be drawn from any period or source whatever; the logic of the matrix, taken as the given, is our only guide in the selection of illustrative events. Once again, in spite of all the precautions we can a

14. Cf. "The Concept of Cultural Classicism," (*Mod. Isl.*, pp. 98-128. If we relate what is said in this paper to the special case of Islam, we must logically reach the formula: classicism = tradition. Von Grunebaum's remarks about classicism in the limited sense that is applicable to literature do nothing to clarify the subject.

priori assume that a serious investigator has taken, we cannot dismiss the suspicion of subjectivism that dogs the entire undertaking.

3. Because decadence is implicit in the very definition of tradition,[15] the problems of decadence as such disappear. One can certainly speak of attenuating or aggravating circumstances that precipitate or delay decadence, but the real cause is in the matrix, the principle of exclusion that is also the principle of identity. Every culture, being a closed system structured by a choice, is eventually doomed to stagnation and sterile repetition.[16] Once tradition has been formulated, it is condemned to reformulate itself again and again, with ever narrower limits and increasing sterility. We find here a distant consequence of the idea of an "end to history." Therefore, properly speaking, there is neither a decadent Islam nor a modern Islam.[17] In von Grunebaum's view, the question we should ask about modern Islam is this: Is there maintenance or abandonment of the fundamental principle? Is there cultural continuity or a winding up, which in turn marks the beginning of another culture? Modern Islam is a

15. Thus we reach the following equation: Islam = unitary principle = classicism = tradition = decadence. The formative period (sixth to ninth centuries) is confused and, at the same time, creative. Modern Islam also is a period of confusion, but it is a negative one, for its keynote is denial. To set oneself apart when self-knowledge has been achieved is necessarily to stagnate. This is the meaning of the article "La convergence des traditions culturelles en Méditerranée," which contains many hard judgments on Arab nationalism; according to von Grunebaum, nationalism seeks to differentiate itself on the basis of what is already given, not on the basis of what could be. The latter course was taken by Islam in its formative period.

16. Regarding the modern West (and this is an important point), von Grunebaum seems to think that it possesses a remarkable privilege in that, for the first time, we see a culture making a tradition of anti-tradition (stagnation is death). The West, therefore, cannot die except by accident or renunciation *(Mod. Isl.,* p. 96).

17. In *Classical Islam* (London, 1970) von Grunebaum stops at the destruction of Baghdad; in "Islamic Literature" *(op. cit.)* he notes the importance of Napoleon's expedition to Egypt, but this has no influence on his views. Examples are taken indiscriminately from all periods.

geographical denotation: it is the world that used to be the domain of Islam, a world whose experience today is, and has been for the past century, one of utter intellectual disorder. The numerous studies that von Grunebaum has devoted to nationalism, to acculturation, to Westernization, and to Muslim self-interpretation, all boil down to this: Islam today denies the West because it remains faithful to its fundamental aspiration but cannot undergo modernization unless it reinterprets itself from the Western point of view and accepts the Western idea of man and the Western definition of truth. Hence the importance he accords to the study of historiography.[18]

4. In principle, no culture that has been materialized in a tradition can renew itself. Novelty may be aimed at or postulated but can no longer be actualized, either by the traditionalists, who have no desire for it, or by the liberal adapters, or by the modernists, who, without conceding the fact, accept the inevitable when it is already a fait accompli. The first of these groups does not see that Islam has already solved all the problems it was able to solve; the second group is par excellence respectful toward the West, and the third fails to understand that cultural traditions do not integrate without reason. Lengthy references to German or Russian experience[19] are designed to show that Islam—refusals, con-

18. Cf. *Isl.*, pp. 184-185. He takes up on his own account H. A. R. Gibb's assertion that he has not seen a single book written by an Arab that makes it possible for the Western student, or even for Arabs themselves, to understand the roots of Arab culture. Von Grunebaum extends this statement to include the non-Arab Muslim and his failure to interpret his culture either to himself or to the West. He adds that this incapacity is likely to hold good for some time, because the traditional Muslim fails to think of his civilization as one among several whose differences in structure result in differences of possibilities and values. We have here an implicit definition of the "culturalist" method as the only scientific method.

19. Cf. *Mod. Isl.*, pp. 347, n. 16; 336, n. 42. Von Grunebaum makes an interesting comparison between the Slavophile thinkers and the spokesmen for Arab nationalism. They have in common a romanticism, a utopianism, and an ambivalence of attitude toward Western Europe; also, they both tend to conduct monologues with themselves rather than dialogues with others.

tradictions, confusions, and complexes notwithstanding—
innovates nothing.

Revolt is not creative; likewise, acceptance. Hence von
Grunebaum is opposed to Toynbee's syncretistic vision.[20] To
be sure, he leaves a door open, but one that is overly remin-
iscent of a certain cosmopolitanism that is traditional among
central European intellectuals and does not square entirely
with the "culturalist" method. The only example he offers of
successful Westernization—India—is not very convincing,[21]
and it is difficult to escape the impression that it is not the
Islamist who is speaking here, but the aesthete admirer of
Thomas Mann and the fellow countryman of Musil.

The foregoing remarks are intended to show what conclusions are implicit in, and must necessarily devolve from, von
Grunebaum's method—conclusions that in turn give rise to
descriptive value judgments. I have not taken a critical
attitude: self-indulgence in this direction can too easily lead
to the dismissal of every scientific undertaking. These days
we are sufficiently aware of the epistemological presuppositions of the social sciences, and even the natural sciences, to
know that formal criticisms of this kind are completely
inadequate. In the same way, a pragmatic critique that asks,
Can these analyses provide us with the blueprint for a
workable polity in the Muslim countries? would also be
inadmissible, for von Grunebaum explicitly states that his
works aim in the main at an introspection of Western
culture.[22]

20. "In brief, Islam is not likely to lose itself in Western civilization
to the extinction of its own 'personality,' even though it may use the
foreign stimulus as a lever for its own revitalization." (Isl., p. 244.)
21. Mod. Isl., p. 389. He cites Nirad Chaudhuri, author of The
Autobiography of an Unknown Indian (New York, 1951), as an
example of success. Yet one could not find a better example of
complete intellectual alienation than this book.
22. "And there may be no better guide to our own soul than the
civilization which a great French scholar has called 'The Occident of
the East,' the world of Islam." (Exp. Hol., p. 27.)

VI

A serious critique must be founded upon a methodological choice; that much is evident. It should also remain within the framework of accepted epistemological rules. We may examine von Grunebaum's "culturalist" presuppositions in their generality, certainly, and in their applicability to Islam, but in doing so we must not forget to submit to the laws of modern historiography. Before contesting his conclusions we should make clear that we recognize von Grunebaum's right to his position. If we do not, he will justifiably maintain that he alone possesses objectivity. At this level of criticism, we must accept a certain division of labor:[23] sociologist must answer sociologist, and historian must answer historian, according to the rules of the game; a special place will remain (as we shall see) for the theologian and the moralist. But we must not continue to confuse the domains, to have one law for oneself and another for one's opponent[24]—a habit that in my opinion has been the principal weakness of the *salafī* movement in all its forms, and that will always condemn as inadequate the thinking that has not made the essential choice between objectivity and subjectivity, between the discursive and the intuitive, between what is universally applicable and what is true from a particular standpoint only.

Having said this, what are our objections to von Grunebaum's point of view?

I have already implied in the preceding sections that the analyses of cultural anthropology—even when it defines its own boundaries (as it has the right to do) within a special area of study, thus voluntarily restricting its scope so that it

23. In and of itself, this division of labor reveals a profound transformation of society and State.
24. Cf. the judgment on Abūʾl-Ḥasan an-Nadwī: "It is a peculiar cultural provincialism to which Nadwī gives vent, peculiar in the sense that his Islam is located in a no man's land outside history, even though he would have us discover it in the age of the first four successors to the Prophet." *(Mod. Isl.,* p. 252.)

may aim at achieving limited but significant results—involve too many distortions, reductions, and subjectivist confusions for it to keep, as von Grunebaum hopes it will, a central position among the social sciences.[25] The failure can be brought back to one cause: an impoverishment of the concept of history.

Cultural anthropology has doubtless evolved from historicism, but it retains all the faults imputable to its romantically inspired origins. History is continually appealed to; but in reality it is replaced for the most part by a theory of history that is little more than a very poorly conceived sketch. So many problems are dismissed from the start as false, so many conclusions are devaluated, so many conclusions are implicit in the premises that it is difficult to see how the outlook of cultural anthropology could possibly encourage concrete research.

Let us briefly consider the idealist parti pris that regards a certain choice among possible choices as the informing principle of a culture. Insofar as no concrete element preponderates, and insofar as the structure at the end of the process is inferred from a choice for which history alone (such as it is interpreted) is answerable, we are clearly dealing with an idealist determinism that, severed from its Hegelian roots, is ultimately without explanatory value, even if it facilitates a certain understanding. It is possible, certainly, to appeal to the example of the natural sciences—and such appeals are not lacking—in order to show that one's own method is not fundamentally different and the results not dissimilar except insofar as the constructed "objects" of the two categories of science are dissimilar. But consistency demands that the example of the natural sciences should be followed also in this: an hypothesis that can be maintained only by increasingly restricting the field of study or distorting the observed

25. "It is my contention that for our time cultural anthropology, understood as human self-analysis by means of a *Kulturlehre* (*Kulturanalyse*), holds the key position in the organization of sciences." (*Mod. Isl.*, p. 50.)

facts must be abandoned. Now, von Grunebaum's cultural anthropology does indeed result in such restrictions and distortions.

This is particularly apparent when we come to Islamic *science*, which manifestly embarrasses our author,[26] and this for two reasons: because of its very existence, which does not square with the apparent unitary principle of Islam, and because of the famous problem of its influence upon Europe. Others had already observed that the evolution of Islamic science did not at all coincide with that of society or State: the great scientific discoveries took place during periods of political decadence and social confusion. This evolution is in fact largely unexplored and would certainly shed light on many facts, hitherto little understood, that are related to Islamic society and culture. Now, von Grunebaum devaluates the importance to his subject of both science and research, and appeals to a theory of truth that he considers a central, informing principle of Islam. He concludes that, in any case, science could have been only marginal and was bound to peter out, for it was founded upon an inadequate theory of knowledge. But the situation was no different in Western Europe until the seventeenth century and probably beyond.[27] Moreover, no account is taken of the autonomy of the caste of scholars. Who can say that the dominating ideology (the theory of truth) was the one prevailing among Muslim savants?[28] To shackle the "truth" of the theologians to the

26. "We are inclined to admire medieval scholars who broke the limitations that theology as the highest of sciences imposed on the rational investigation of the universe. With due respect to their intellectual boldness, the question cannot always be brushed aside whether those innovators had any *right* to their departure from the established system." (*Med. Isl.*, p. 331. Italics supplied.)

27. Let us recall the recent discussions on the "philosophy" of the Renaissance, which was in fact less "scientific" than that of the late Middle Ages. One has only to think of Giordano Bruno, Paracelsus, and the massive revival of magic.

28. See M. Mahdi, "Remarks on the Theologus Autodidactus of Ibn al-Nafīs," *St. Isl.*, XXXI, 1970.

practice of savants only makes us blind to the real consecutions—the chains of events that allowed the development, the
maintenance and the stagnation of Islamic science. Here we
see clearly how a theory of history impoverishes real history
and inhibits research in an important area. To say that
Islamic science was in any case condemned to come to
nothing by no means explains why Ibn al-Nafīs, working in
freedom, was forgotten, while on the contrary Galileo, who
was harassed, was remembered. To say that Islamic science
was an external grafting is no more satisfactory, since there
is too long an interval between the period of the original
graft and that (for example) of Ibn al-Nafīs.

The same reservation applies to the studies of the numerous
periods of decadence in Islamic history, all of which are
different: the decadence of the Mamlūks, the Moghuls, the
Ottomans, the ʿAlawites, etc. Who will be satisfied to reduce
them all to an abstract model, that of the ʿAbbāsids or the
Seljūqs? For, from the standpoint of cultural anthropology,
the problem is reversed: it seeks to know the reasons for
persistence rather than the reasons for decadence. Von
Grunebaum expresses this problem at least once,[29] and
can find no convincing answer (unless we consider that
recourse to individualistic fatalism is convincing). Then
there is the question of modern Islam. To define it only
by its composite character is too descriptive. Von Grunebaum subscribes to W. Cantwell Smith's opinion that
only the Turks among all the Muslims have definitely
adopted the point of view of Western historiography. But
why they and not the Arabs? Because it is a matter
of choice, the author seems to say. Whether it arrives
early or late it will always be inexplicable to the deter-
ministic understanding, so that the time taken to make

---

29. "In the light of the crudeness of [Islam's] origin its achievement
is extraordinary, and the tenacious vitality of this civilization, whose
answers to the elemental questions besetting the human mind still
satisfy about one-eighth of mankind, is indeed a cause for wonder."
(*Med. Isl.*, p. 346.)

the choice is considered by him to be unimportant.[30] This is a priori to give tremendous sway to the champions of explicit traditionalism, but the Islam of today holds more than the *ʿulamā* and the professional apologists, even if it is necessary to recognize that the *aggiornamento* of the *ʿulamā* is and will be of the highest importance. Von Grunebaum delimits the area of contradictions, but he goes no further; here we see a devaluation of real history and above all an admission that culture is inadequate to explain culture, whether in crisis or in self-transcendence.[31]

Finally, let me add that the process of constructing the matrix of Islam leaves one with an impression of extreme subjectivism. I use the term "impression" advisedly; I am aware that it is always possible to retort that such an impression emerges only during the final stage of the presentation and is preceded by a more systematic investigation during the research stage. Bearing this in mind, we are nevertheless nonplussed by the eclecticism of the examples and quotations. This, while it bears witness to an unusual breadth of knowledge, does not help to create a sense of conviction. Cultural analysis wished to systematize the facts in order that a traditional pointillism might be avoided, and here we already see it on the verge of a new eclecticism. When all is said and done, does the fundamental choice of a culture amount only to the personal choice of the analyst?

All these criticisms would be empty if von Grunebaum—despite, or because of, these restrictions, reductions, and comparisons—actually succeeded in isolating this "structuring principle." In the course of reading his numerous and often subtle analyses, we are made aware of a large number of concordances, continuities, and contrasts, which are all

30. See *Isl.*, p. 230. A new Islamic self-interpretation requires acceptance of the Western attitude to reality, "which is at the bottom of its scientific control of nature," and acceptance of the spirit of free criticism.
31. See *Isl.*, p. 244. Nationalism is a cause of retardation in cultural self-consciousness, historical research, etc. But how does one account for nationalism in the first place?

intended to direct our attention toward a common origin; it is
precisely here that the deception begins. If we take the texts
that deal most explicitly with this subject—the conclusion of
Medieval Islam, the chapter in *Islam* entitled "The Profile of
Muslim Civilization," and the chapter in *Modern Islam*
entitled "An Analysis of Islamic Civilization and Cultural
Anthropology"—we detect four principal characteristics:
antihumanism; the truth as a revealed absolute; personality
as something static, obedient, and calm; and a particular style
or tone.[32] This last point has no heuristic value, and the
three others come down finally to a choice of God over man.
The question is not whether this aspiration is really that of
Sunnī Islam; rather, it is a question of seeing that it is too
great a generality really to define Islam. This is clearly seen
when von Grunebaum tries to define Arab culture, or when
he is characterizing all premodern cultures,[33] for he gives us
no means of isolating Islam from the premodern cultures or
Arab culture from Islam. In short, we have here a quasi-
equation: Islam = culture = Arab culture = the negative
of modern culture. In reality, the agreements and contrasts
are between the modern West and premodern cultures.

32. "It is essential to realize that Muslim civilization is a cultural
entity that does not share our primary aspirations. It is not vitally
interested in analytical self-understanding, and it is even less interested in the structural study of other cultures, either as an end in
itself or as a means toward clearer understanding of its own
character and history. . . . One may perhaps seek to connect it with
the basic antihumanism of this civilization, that is, the determined
refusal to accept man to any extent whatever as the arbiter or the
measure of things, and the tendency to be satisfied with the truth as
the description of mental structures, or, in other words, with
psychological truth." *(Mod. Isl.,* p. 55) "The strength of Islam is in
the roundedness of personality which at its best it is able to
produce." *(Med. Isl.,* p. 346.) "To [the Muslim investigator] the
sciences were fundamentally a stable system of formal and material
truths communicated to man for safekeeping in what we should call
prehistoric times." *(Ibid.,* p. 328.) "[Islam's] flavor is unmistakable
on whatever it touched" *(Ibid.,* p. 324.)
33. Cf. *Isl.,* pp. 58-77, for Arab culture, and *Le Rêve* . . . , pp. 8 and
9. "All civilizations before Descartes are medieval, premodern."

Thus the particular analyses, notwithstanding their wealth of illustration, are incommensurable with the conclusions, which simply reproduce the presuppositions of the method. Culture defined as a principle of organization and differentiation, and Islam defined as culture—both of these are postulates, and remain so after the analysis. Cultural anthropology is indeed a philosophy; it is far from being a means of discovery and of scientific investigation. In this there is nothing invalidating, and von Grunebaum, faithful to his historicist inspiration, would doubtless maintain the avowed privilege of the West on the basis of cultural anthropology *qua* philosophy, for he would claim that this philosophy is a uniquely Western aspiration toward self-knowledge, a feature that distinguishes it from all other cultures.[34] It is even possible that Islam will take this philosophy on its own account, as it has taken many things before—all the more so as it is a philosophy that includes many genuinely scientific elements. It is these that account for its persistent influence.

Our task is to isolate these genuinely scientific elements and to point to the larger methodological framework in which they may be integrated.

VII

I have already said that the preceding critique, or any other critique for that matter, is admissible only if one is willing to accept for oneself the principle of modern historiography, namely, the conception of truth as an indefinite process. In these circumstances, and given shared procedural aproaches,

34. "All we shall really have time to do is to leave to our successors convincing samples of our kind of perceptiveness and of the kind of truth to which it has led us. Our methodology will not be lost, but many of our results and much of our manner of presentation will imperceptibly but inevitably turn into source material from which those who come after us will recapture our aspirations, as we are now attempting to recapture the aspirations of those before and around us." *(Mod. Isl.,* p. 96.)

there will inevitably be points of convergence and even similarities of method; there will also, however, be differences of objective that should be fully clarified.

The essential divergence concerns the concept of history. I believe in *not* reducing real history (the burgeoning of different categories of events, different meanings, within a unique temporal experience) to culture. Similarly, culture may not be reduced to ideology, i.e., the theoretical formulation thereof that is continually put forward; and ideology in its turn may not be reduced to theology, which is itself a restrictive theory of the relationship between man and God. This is valid for Islam, as it is valid for any other historio-geographical area.[35] It is perfectly legitimate to isolate the study of culture as an autonomous domain with a particular temporality, but it is not legitimate to claim that this temporality is alone normative.

It should be realized, on the other hand, that the will to systematize is justified, and that to maintain the richness of real history does not entail acceptance of the "pseudologic" of positivist factual history. The latter takes confusion of facts for an empirical systematization, and it fails to see that the temporality that it makes use of as a reference point is itself an artificial construction. Thus the quotidian temporality, the everyday run of political events, imposes itself upon other temporalities—economic, sociopolitical, cultural, ideological, psychosociological, etc.—and even when the professional historian is writing economic history or discussing historical ethos, he does not take care to isolate the particular temporalities of these domains. Everything is dissolved in an apparent intelligibility which is that of the event. It is because the spurious aspect of this intelligibility has long been apparent that the philosophies of history were born. Later tendencies, such as historicism, "sociologism," cultural an-

35. One might indeed maintain that it is this possibility of reduction that individualizes Islam. Von Grunebaum does not expressly say so, but we may infer it from many other of his opinions. One could, however, make the same assertion about any past society whatever, and it would seem impossible either to confirm or to refute it. In this sense the ethnologists' reconstructions do not escape ethnocentricity.

thropology, and "epistemologism,"[36] which all seek a point of departure other than that of the political event, aim at achieving a less simplistic conception of history through the revealing of a particular temporality. This endeavor becomes mistaken when the temporality in question is decreed to be alone real, and science disintegrates into philosophy. If one is careful not to go this far, the undertaking remains perfectly legitimate. What gives it still more validity in the context of Islamic history is that studies that are admittedly confined to limited areas (they are for the most part concerned with language, literature, theology, and historiography) do tend to corroborate an impression in the mind of the historian that the cultural temporality was in fact dominant during a certain period. In order that we may construct an image that is faithful to our insight, we are virtually forced to make use of the idea of an articulated system. Let us be precise: coming automatically, as it were, to the mind, this image remains no more than an image. In and of itself, systematism does not provide sufficient explanatory grounds; justification for the image is to be found in another domain, in another temporality, that is moreover largely unamenable to investigation in the field of Islam. This is *factual history*, which is not negative-critical history or programmatic history, and which remains and will always remain our central concern; it is from the study of factual history that all progress ultimately comes. Naturally, we cannot expect everything to stop until the distant day when factual history will be able to answer all our questions.[37] The other areas must be studied according to their internal logic.

36. The last is represented today by M. Foucault. R. Aron aptly recalls the methodological ties between Foucault and Dilthey: *D'une sainte famille à l'autre* (Paris, 1969), p. 259.
37. This is the objection raised by many critics against the study of contemporary Arab ideological movements. "Since you recognize," they seem to be saying, "the primacy of the economic factor, concern yourself with economic history and leave ideology alone." Thus (for they themselves are not prepared to study economic history), they indefinitely postpone actual research in the name of an ideal situation.

It is, of course, difficult to overstress that the history of
Islam is in this respect seductive and dangerous. Seductive
because it calls for system and structure; everything comes to
us in a framework of culture and ideology: we have a theory
of religion and few evidences of the actual lived religion, a
political theory and few political documents, a theory of
history and few specific dates, a theory of social structure and
few indications of actual social behavior, an economic theory
and few series of economic data, etc.[38] We are in constant
danger of confusing theory with fact: the one is readily
available, while the other demands research and elaboration.
It is this situation that confers an appearance of truth on the
analyses of cultural anthropology; for the temporality they
postulate conforms with the temporality that the Islamic
tradition has itself imposed. We ourselves sometimes have to
be—or appear to be—"culturalists"; but it is our part never
to forget that this temporality—that of tradition and the
"culturalist" analysis that seems to conform so well with it—is
no more than a formulation and is not the naked reality.
The formal agreement between several facts and their reduction to a common meaning may well provide the "culturalist"
with a heuristic construct, but it is not an explanation of
these facts; the factor determining this agreement does not
belong to the culture itself. We must demonstrate this where
we can; where we are not yet able to, we must draw attention
to the assumptions that have been made.[39]

This refusal to reduce history to its theory, while it
legitimizes partial systematizations, results in a conceptual

38. For example, Reuben Levy's book, *Social Structure of Islam*
(Cambridge, 1962), analyzes a normative and theoretical social
structure rather than an actual structure.
39. The analyses of *L'Idéologie arabe contemporaine* (Paris, 1967)
admittedly resemble those of the cultural anthropologists, but those
who read a Hegelian idealism into the book are missing the point:
such a perspective, which is in fact the perspective of the ideologists
themselves, is no more than a phase of the book's overall argument.
I have never stated that ideological evolution is the foundation of
social evolution; I *have* said that at a given moment (for reasons that
are outside the scope of the book) ideological contradictions become
important, if not determinative.

differentiation: structure is not a priori an isomorphic reflection; culture is not the primordial choice between possible
developments; rather, it is the ensemble of cultural artifacts,
whether or not all of these can be presently systematized.
Correspondence or symbolic reduction is not a determination; it is accounted for by the imposition of a determining
element alien to the culture in question. To be sure, this
divergence in the use of ideas will not at first be visible; in
certain developments, above all in those concerned with the
ideology of culture (theories of poetry, God, grammar), the
use of the same procedural means (comparisons pointing to
resemblances or differences; the identification of breaks—
coupures—and reorganizations of the conceptual whole; the
tracking down of a series of possible manifestations, in different areas, of one and the same principle, etc.) may make
this difference seem almost imperceptible. It is at this level
that we may return to many of von Grunebaum's astound-
ingly erudite analyses. For this remains the sole method that
allows us to escape from our endemic evils: eclecticism and
immediate identification with the subjectivity of the past. It
is also the sole means of achieving a certain objectivity, which
is admittedly not the same thing as absolute truth, but which
is the basis of mutual understanding; for we can no longer
impose our tradition, which was our form of objectivity, on
others.[40]

VIII

Given these premises, there will necessarily be division of
labor among those who study Islamic countries. By way of a
preliminary outline, we shall distinguish the four following
domains:

1. Islam as history. At this level, Islam has a geohistorical
meaning only. Every diversity must be taken into considera-

40. As examples of extreme subjectivism, let me cite the numerous
studies by Abū Zahra on the history of the *fiqh* and the studies by
Shawqī Diaf on literature. If we do not succeed in detecting
differences and systematizing them, we shall always be subject to the
eternal present.

tion,[41] and the key concept that will guide research in this area is that of specificity. We must detect the slightest distinguishing characteristics and must never blanket concrete situations with a typical situation; hence we must mistrust all partis pris, whether those of past tradition or those of modern theoreticians. As modern historiography demands, the evolution of economy and culture must be recognized as obeying a different rhythm than that of polity.

2. Islam as "culture." The goal here is the search for a principle that reorganizes cultural manifestations through a process of continual traditionalization. But, unlike the "culturalists," we are not obliged to postulate that the required principle is identical with the traditionalists'. We can reject this kind of historicism and consider it possible that the structuring principle has remained out of reach—the efforts of the traditionalists notwithstanding. Since this reorganization is not in any case determinant, but aims only at reconstructing the most faithful possible image of a structured ensemble of facts, it is quite conceivable that we can now reorganize—better than the traditionalists themselves can—the tradition in question. From this, however, we draw no conclusions: neither that this always implicit structure was the true driving force behind the evolution of Islam, nor that it is the ultimate goal of research.[42] Acceptance of the

41. Cf. *Isl.*, p. 203. Muḥ. Kurd ʿAlī's refusal to consider an Islam in general—it is a different phenomenon in different places and at different times—is entirely justified, and von Grunebaum is entirely unjustified in rejecting it, even if it is affirmed in an apologetic work.
42. The historicism of *L'idéologie* . . . is different from that of the cultural anthropologists because it is induced and limited. Because our society is dominated, the ideological structures upon which I attempt to shed some light are referred to Western history. If our ideologies are themselves ideologically determined, I did not say that the same was true for the West; socioeconomic determination is referred to the West precisely because of the imperialist domination. The exposition is only apparently Hegelian, for it is partial. What the book denies is the fiction that all societies are equal and autonomous in the eyes of "scientific" methodology; this is really a scientific positivism that fails to see the relative unity of the world that has resulted from modern imperialism.

manifold wealth of concrete history frees the elaboration of Islam's cultural system for every possibility of development. Not to confuse history with the theory of history saves the one and liberates the other.

3. Islam as behavior or morality. It is difficult to deny that there exists an educational background, essentially familial, that is common to all the Muslim countries and contributes to the emergence of a traditional personality type, which even today is largely in the majority. Here is a fruitful field of research for the psychosociologist and the psychoanalyst. The analysis of historical individualities, autobiographies, literary models, child psychology, the philosophy of traditional education, family morality, etc., already allows us, and will allow us increasingly in the future, to discern the fundamental structure of the "Muslim personality;" it is in the pluralist societies, if convincing results are desired, that the comparative analysis should be most rigorously pursued.[43] But here again, if we are obliged to delimit theoretically the domain in which psychoanalysis and historical psychology are adequate to their objects, we a priori affirm nothing; we do not deduce this behavior, this psychology or personality, from a theological theory; rather, we deduce from it the possibility of the family's autonomy in relation to society, and hence the possibility of its particular temporality. This personality is not an object of study except inasmuch as history itself has allowed us to isolate it. It can be considered neither the goal (or meaning) of evolution nor its origin (or reason). We should always distrust the tendency to use such a personality as a means of explaining the development of factual history. It may well be that, in certain conditions, this "solidified equilibrium" (Gestalt) that is a stable personality type could have a determining influence on political, social,

43. Cf., on this point, Cheikh Hamidou Kane, *L'Aventure ambiguë* (Paris, 1961), and Taha Husayn's *Al-Ayyām* (Days). It is evident that it is in countries like India, Lebanon, and Nigeria that promising studies of Muslim psychology could be made, for in these countries there is a significant narrowing of the range of differences between Muslim and non-Muslim groups.

or even economic evolution, but again it is history in all its complexity that accounts for the realization of this possibility.

4. Islam as faith. This is the most difficult area to isolate in the framework of actual research. Since everything that is normative *(fiqh)*, theoretical (theology), or ethical (personality) belongs to other domains, we can demarcate this area by simply looking for what remains unanalyzed. Here again, the Orientalist and the traditionalist are on common ground when they state that Islam per se is in fact confined to the preceding categories; for the former, there are no other categories;[44] for the latter, what remains is the ineffable. That attitude (very widespread among ideologists), which consists in identifying oneself directly with a certain facet of tradition and in using it to reorganize the past, present, and future of the totality or of part of the Islamic world, is not within the scope of what we are trying to define. Rather, it forms part of present-day Muslim ideology and should be analyzed in the context of area 1 (Islam as history). We can candidly state that the present time sees few attempts to elucidate Islam qua faith. Explanations of this fact could be multiplied; it is enough to stress the undeniable role played by the methodological confusion I have attempted to dispel.

The division of labor, such as I have outlined above, is at once dictated by the exigencies of science and a concern for practical results. To each it will guarantee great freedom in his chosen field of study, as much for Muslims as for non-Muslims. Each will know, and will have good grounds for knowing, what he can and what he cannot do. The foregoing methodological choices can be represented thus:

1. History
2. Behavior
3. Culture
4. Faith

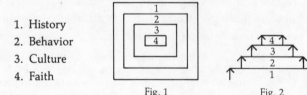

Fig. 1   Fig. 2

44. Von Grunebaum emphasizes the importance of outward practices (prayer, fasting, alms, pilgrimage) in the definition of Islam, which thus begins to bear a resemblance to the religion of the Law.

Figure 1 represents the methodological choice of the Orientalist and the traditionalist; 4, representing the domain of the sacred, which leads down to ʿaqīda, to fiqh, and to behavior, is the heart of the whole system, the driving force and the determining factor. Figure 2, on the other hand, delimits research domains as levels of particular temporalities, but each level is determined by its predecessor. This is not to say there is no conformation of one level to the succeeding level; there is a big step, however, from determination to conformation; momentary reversals of the direction of determination can occur—the effect can become a cause—but these have to be demonstrated and explained by empirical research in the specific areas concerned.

IX

I would like to add a few concluding remarks about domain 4, which is the most difficult to demarcate. A possible point of departure would be a rethinking of the notion of Minhāj al-sunna: a re-examination of the logical substructure of the sunna (or of Shiʿism, Ibāḍism, or the semi-Shiʿism that is found in certain countries.[45] It is not a question of reconstructing the historical development of the Sunnī ʿaqīda—that falls within the province of 1, and, at another level, of 2—but rather of making the Sunnites say what they tried to say without altogether succeeding.[46] The Sunnites thought in terms of means and ends; the means of elucidation and proof changed but were all put to the service of one and the same end. Our concern now is to see what rationale and meaning resided in this end, and it is this that we should identify. He

45. The Sunnism of Morocco, for example, has unique characteristics that are not to be found even in neighboring countries.
46. This interpretation is possible vis-à-vis all discourse, even that situated at the most conscious level. It is the passage of time that draws the conscious toward the unconscious, and it is legitimate to speak of the discourse or the rationale of revolution without implying that this rationale was its essence or its hidden truth. Rather, it is *our* truth that is in question, which of course depends on something other than our subjectivity.

who formulates what he will call (according to his conceptual framework) a new theology, or a new analysis, or a new interpretation of the faith, will not of course be thinking in terms of today but of always. He will aim at what was being communicated through—and in spite of—theological systems.

At this level also history will be present, but indirectly, in the form of the difficulties, problems, and antinomies that confront the conscious man of faith. The ideologist who identifies immediately with tradition devaluates these difficulties by his adherence; he is illuminated, and everything is transvalued. Whereas, on the level at which we are trying to stay, the man of faith justifies problems as such. Here are some of them:

——The ⁽aqīda of the past are to be reinterpreted. This of course entails a break *(coupure)*. The historian and the cultural anthropologist will see in this only a total rupture; but the man of faith, from his perspective, will see no essential difference of quality between his reinterpretation and those effected by al-Ash⁽arī, Ghazzālī, Ibn Taimiyya, and others. What is more, he will insist that this break is implied in the act of faith of each Muslim.[48]

——Faith in general, the very concept of faith, will have to be thought out anew. The need is for an inclusive theory that will combine the appearances, degrees, stages, etc., of faith; for the resistance of others and their unwillingness to listen is a fact—both within Islam and without. Denial of this fact will

47. See the interesting attempt by Hasan Hanafi, *Les Méthodes d'exégèse* (Cairo, 1965), and "Théologie ou Anthropologie," *Renaissance du monde arabe* (Brussels, 1972), pp. 233-264, where he states that theology is not religion, and adds (p. 246): "Jurisprudence may serve as a courageous model for the transformation of religion, not into theology, but into anthropology."
48. "Writing is the renewal of history." ("Théologie ou Anthropologie," *op. cit.*, p. 255.) "Religious thought is in essence formless thought. Its form comes from history. . . . The project develops in a radical spirit. Its aim is put an end to tradition for ever so that religion may become part of developing reality." *(Ibid.*, p. 261.) "In this sense mystics are the true interpreters of religion and theologians the false." *(Ibid.*, p. 262.)

impress nobody except those whose faith is still unrational-
ized, and unconsciousness of this kind is becoming increasingly rare. And if we are unwilling to face the realities of the
situation, we fall into "false consciousness"; that is, we
become a category or a moment in a theory of faith that is
not our own.[49]

Society, in all its complexity and at all levels, is to be taken
as a given fact that imposes itself upon the man of faith; it is
not deducible from the norms he prescribes for it. To
postulate the contrary is to fall back into the ideological
thinking that forms part of domain 1. At the level of consciousness we are discussing, the man of faith must depart
from the principle that he can no longer decisively influence
the problems of political power; on the contrary, it is the very
condition of his enterprise. If it is not, he has no recourse but
to await the return of utopia and say nothing. And this is not
because he is weak, but because the modern concept of faith
contains the principle in question. The elaboration or elucidation here being envisaged will necessarily be the achievement
of a heroic minority; but it is in this framework alone that
an Islam for the present time may be born.

The realization of the preceding formal conditions does not
depend (as can easily be inferred from the expositions that
prepared the ground) on the formulation of faith itself, nor on
behavior, nor on culture, but on the evolution of history in all

49. Von Grunebaum takes up A. L. Kroeber's idea that Islam is a
reduction and a simplification of the credo of the period, this being
essentially Christian (Med. Isl., p. 7), and adds that it will never
make up its conceptual retardation (Med. Isl., p. 322). Christian
theology, taken as a whole, includes Islam at least as a possibility,
whereas Islam could never have included all the potentialities of
Christian theology; whence von Grunebaum's unfavorable judgment
on Ibn Ḥazm's position, which could be invoked against him. It
must be said, however, that one should not attempt to rebut this
with an apparatus of historiographical research (show him, for
example, that in the tenth century Muslim theology was superior to
Christian theology). The only true answer will consist in the
reinterpretation of Islam as faith. Otherwise the present will always
justify him.

its sinuous complexity. That the reformulation of faith is a consequence of this evolution need hardly be emphasized; this will not be verified, however, until the end of the process. If this were not so, we should have to conclude with a banality: inasmuch as a fact is not fulfilled, it is because the conditions of its fulfillment have not yet been achieved. The reformulation actually depends on subjective conditions that are not always accountable to a single society; its social impact and propagation are always dependent, on the other hand, on objective factors. It is very possible that this reformulation of faith is presently the preoccupation of some unknown person whom glory awaits. Once again we shall witness a formal verification of the proposition, "Islam is for all times," precisely because it is never the same Islam; the word quite simply designates a reality that is always being renewed.[50] The historian, the anthropologist, the social analyst have nothing to say at this level of interpretation; it is for the man of faith to speak while they listen and record.

50. It is here that the necessity for an analytical study of the Arabic language as mirror of eternity makes itself felt. But we must go beyond this study even while we make it. We must explain why the language aids the illusion of eternity; but there is no need to commit ourselves to a literal quest for the eternal and transcendent, as the linguistic "philosophers" seem to do. We are well aware that grammar, theology, and tradition are intimately linked in Islam, and we understand the kind of fascination exerted by those structuralist tendencies that are farthest from rigorous scientific objectivity. But along that way lies a return to tradition, and the great detour via the preciosities of modern linguistics is superfluous. While the autonomy of linguistic science must be fully recognized, it is precisely my contention that we should strip the illusion that consists in taking the language as a mirror of eternity—an illusion that lies near the heart of all the aesthetic, theological, and epistemological problems of our traditional culture. The reinterpretation alluded to in the preceding note must *not* take the Arabic language as its basis, or it will ineluctably meet with the traditional mystique.

II

HISTORICISM AND MODERNIZATION

4

HISTORICISM AND THE ARAB INTELLIGENTSIA

We are philosophical contemporaries of the present
without being its historical contemporaries.
Karl Marx, "Toward a Critique of Hegel's Philosophy
of Right."

Philosophy is born, develops, and lives again in polemic. It is
not by re-examining old problems with the old terminology
that it can save itself from ever-threatening anachronism; it
renews itself only by occupying itself with the questions that
are the stuff of everyday social practice, and these first appear
in the form of critical polemic. It took time to appreciate that
Lenin had raised formidable ethical and epistemological
problems in the short occasional writings in which he had
criticized his comrades of the Russian Social Democratic
party in the years from 1900 to 1910; likewise, we have not
yet exhausted the wealth of material contained in the debates
that divided Western Marxism in Berlin, Vienna, or Budapest
during the period of the German Revolution (1920-1924). It
is of course unusual for it to be the protagonists themselves
who draw the most rewarding theoretical conclusions from
these debates. Who today likes to emphasize that the problematics of a Max Weber, a Joseph Schumpeter or a Karl
Mannheim—problematics that were so influential in the
domain of the social sciences—derive with little modification
from the Marxist questioning during those years or the
immediately preceding period? And there are other schools of

formalist inspiration that derive from this seminal polemic. For, has it not been philosophy's perennial temptation ever since Plato to escape from history, from dialectic, and from the event? Yet, it has long been demonstrated (in different cultural contexts) that the renewal of philosophy rarely comes from any source other than reflection on contemporary politics.[1]

Today, if you were to set out to find the refuges of philosophic thinking in the Arab countries, you certainly would not discover them in the peaceful places frequented by philosophy professors, just as you would find few theories of God formulated by the various ʿulamā, faqīhs, and khatībs subsidized by the modern State, or few instances of liberalism among the advocates and journalists. You will certainly find new editions of the philosophical and theological classics, and commentaries thereon, and praiseworthy efforts to keep modern terminology up to date; but you will not find the much-needed guide to the work of a Fārābī or an Ibn Khaldūn that explains the usefulness and relevance of such writers to the present time and prevents us from being dragged by their dead weight into the region of the frozen moment. Still less will you find an antidote to the compartmentalization of heart and mind that estranges the three components of modern Arab culture: the classical Greek heritage as interpreted by the Muslim thinkers, medieval Islamic thought, and modern Western philosophy in all the variety of its successive connotations.

A living integrative system, capable of extirpating the endemic weakness of all old cultures, namely, the eclecticism that is death to thought, is not found today except in one literary category, that of the essay, and especially in those essays that deal with current political events. Modern

1. For classical Arab philosophy and the role played by political concerns in the development of this philosophy, see M. Mahdi's well-documented and scrupulous article, "Islamic Philosophy," in the new edition of the *Encyclopaedia Britannica*.

mutakallimūn, the Arab writers of today, almost never attain to philosophy unless they are actively engaged in polemic.[2]

THE RATIONALE OF THE FIRST *NAHDA*

The long period of struggle for political emancipation, which witnessed a violent and often fluctuating opposition between the modernists and the conservatives, between the supporters of religion and the secularists, between the radicals and the moderates, and whose only permanent feature was a sort of duet played under the foreign dominator's watchful and somewhat ironic eye, has bequeathed us a rich polemical literature that only now is beginning to be the object of methodical studies. Doubtless the problems posed—Why decadence on the one hand and hegemony on the other? How does one accomplish a renaissance? What is the meaning of the Arabs' *mihnah* (ordeal)?—seemed even then, and seem today still more, to be dead letters. Just as an Egyptian naturalistic novel may seem to many Western readers little more than a pale copy of Zola rewritten by Pio Baroja, so may those long dissertations seem like dry summaries of Renaissance or eighteenth-century writers. However, we should go beyond this first evaluation and read, in succession, studies of modern Arab thought, nineteenth-century Russian philosophy, and Chinese thought after 1840:[3] we repeatedly encounter the same structure without the slightest indication of previous entente or mutual influence. Where is their unifying matrix?

2. Nassif Nassar is more of a philosopher in his essay *Naḥwa Mujtamaᶜ Jadīd (Toward a New Society)* (Beirut, 1970), in which he censures the denominational structures of contemporary Lebanon, than in his study of the realist thought of Ibn Khaldūn.

3. For example: Albert Hourani, *Arabic Thought in the Liberal Age* (London, 1962); Hans Kohn, *Panslavism* (New York, 1953); S. Y. Teng and John K. Fairbank, *China's Response to the West* (Cambridge, Mass., 1954). To be added to this list is Octavio Paz's admirable essay, *The Labyrinth of Solitude*. I did not come across this until after I had completed *L'Idéologie*. . . .

It is the West, it will be said. But how are we to define the West, especially when we consider that these essays begin by asking precisely this question—What is the West?—and that behind the objective appearance of the West there lies concealed the accompanying shadow of an anti-West? The West inwardly questions itself even while others question it from without.

The similarity of the progression (or succession) of thoughts (rather than similarities between thinkers)[4] would in itself furnish ample matter for comparisons. Furthermore, all these sequences—taken from different non-Western cultural contexts and brought back to their common problematic—would again confer all their acuity to old but still undecided questions, which, having received formal expression in the past, have perhaps a better chance of being concentrated today.

First, some specific questions relating to the role of the individual—questions that are very intriguing if we are not too free with the hypothesis of individual genius. Why was Bielinski capable of understanding Hegel and not V. Cousin, nor any Englishman of the nineteenth century? How was Lessing able to define the conditions for a new theater and not Diderot? And Herder create a true philosophy of history and not Voltaire? Let us go further: how could Rousseau grasp the incomparable logic of Hobbes and not Locke?[5]

Underlying these are further questions of a general nature. What are the dialectical links between the following concepts: hegemony, tradition, historicism, and revolution? When one speaks (according to country and circumstance) of foreign action or influence, of external pressure, domination, or challenge, is one referring to degrees of development of an identical phenomenon or is one superposing separate phenomena? In the event that the first hypothesis is the more

4. See *L'Idéologie* . . . , *op. cit.*, ch. 2; and *China's Response* . . . , which cites a 1922 text by Liang Ch'i-ch'ao, pp. 267-274.
5. A question that is precisely delineated by E. Cassirer in *The Philosophy of the Enlightenment*, albeit in the framework of formal analysis, that is, of ideas divorced from their sociohistorical context.

correct, what effect has the choice of means: arms, merchandise, or ideas? It is said that economy is a form of war, freedom of trade a form of aggression. It has been observed that Hegel studied English political economy before thinking about Napoleonic expansionism, and it is true that it was not the Decembrists or the savants accompanying Bonaparte's expeditions who overturned societies, whether Russian or Egyptian, but English furniture. Hence it is said that administration by foreigners follows armed force, and ideas infiltrate along the highways of conquest; this has long been believed, and it is believed less and less. Tradition is born in confrontation with military or commercial aggression (some might prefer the terms "neo-tradition" or "retraditionalization". Slavism, *brahmo samaj,* the reinterpretation of Confucius by Kang Yu-wei, *salafiyya*—these responses are doubtless different but nonetheless display the same structure. In re-examining old European responses (all the "neo-isms"), would not the generalization of this problematic permit an evaluation of the specific weight of those dialectical responses, one which will be neither that of unalloyed truth nor that of out-and-out falsity?

Tradition is born in opposition to something: to ideas accompanying foreign merchandise, or to a universally decried liberalism. The non-European liberal has always been taxed with superficiality,[6] and the cry against "imported ideologies" so often heard in Arab countries is by no means new; it was raised in Germany against G. Forster and in numerous Russian novels.[7] One might say that the vitality of historicism has always sprung from this natural opposition. From the outset, historicism serves the purposes of two

6. A. Gramsci writes: "One understands the 'national,' albeit deep import of conservative and reactionary currents, as compared with democratic currents; the latter were extended but superficial— 'flashes in the pan'—where the former were less widespread but more deeply rooted." *(Oeuvres choisies* (Paris, 1959), p. 463.
7. Such is the theory regarding Pushkin in Dostoyevsky's *Pages from the Journal of an Author.* Regarding Forster, see Lukács, *Brève histoire de la littérature allemande* (Paris, 1964).

tendencies: on the one hand conservation and passivity through submission to the facts, and on the other hand action and change. Also from the outset the historicism of conservation rapidly blends with tradition at a higher level of intellectual refinement, whereas activist historicism, or the historicism of the left, goes beyond the internalization of objectivity—the classical attempt to master nature by submission to her laws —and strives to make the leap toward liberty. Activist historicism justifies liberalism (liberalism is incapable of doing this for itself) and thus truly surpasses it, accomplishing an act of transcendence that is affirmed but hardly realized by the historicism of conservation. Marx indeed preferred free trade to economic nationalism, but he reserved his fiercest ideological attacks for John Stuart Mill.[8] Lenin, though his decision in April 1917 may give one cause to think otherwise, always sided with those who were prepared to grant history its real weight as against those who were champions of mere rhetoric—a fact that he unequivocally demonstrated during the NEP.

What finally emerges from the Arab revolutionary ideologist's thinking about his past is a reactualization of historicism in circumstances identical to those in which it saw the light of day. During the nineteenth century, historicism had lost a clearly defined meaning; it became synonymous with historical relativism, with evolutionism, with the theology of history, and even with nihilistic casuistry. But a clear understanding of what historicism had been and what, in given circumstances, it can always be—namely, the inner logic of political action—was forgotten, even when such a wide-ranging intellect as Gramsci's was concerned to reformulate

8. From among a great number of possible sources let me quote one of the clearest definitions of historicism as it is understood in this essay: "And even when a society has got upon the right track for the discovery of the natural laws of its movement . . . it can neither clear by bold leaps, nor remove by legal enactments, the obstacles offered by the successive phases of its normal development. But it can shorten and lessen the birth-pangs." (Author's preface to *Capital*, 1867.) Liberalism believes in fiats, and traditionalist historicism denies the necessity for cutting short the period of gestation.

it. Historiographers, epistemologists, formalists of all kinds and colors, obfuscated by the search for "stable structures," may well announce the poverty or tautology of historicism. They are not seeing it for what it really is: the practice of the modern Prince.[9]

DEVELOPMENTS

Prior to the Second World War, Arab ideologists believed in the evidence of their thought and were scarcely concerned with understanding the nature of their thought processes. Any idea of acting as catalysts for successive generalizations on the subject of world unification, a process conceived as being made possible by a series of resolved contradictions, was far from their minds. This comparison did not come to mind until a center was established in the West whose purpose was to study everything that was not itself. But it

9. L. Goldmann, who is far from being an enemy of historicism, nevertheless defines it in a conventional manner: "The totality of comprehensive positions that admit the necessity for understanding human realities in the total historical context of a period or a civilization—which context implies ends and values—but refuses to introduce objectivity into the theoretical analyses." ("Recherches dialectiques," *Temps modernes*, vol. 140 [Paris,] p. 730). So, by reducing historicism to the banal ideology of the historians, he deprives it of any meaning and effectively impoverishes it. But L. Althusser is not far from doing likewise when he writes: "The basic structure of all historicism: the contemporaneity which makes possible a reading in essential section." (*Reading Capital*, p. 138, with explanations on pp. 131-132). Discussing Gramsci, J. Texier writes: "The philosophy for which all reality is history is called historicism." Karl Popper defines it with regard to its claim to predict the future of a society by imprisoning it in an enclosed totality. (Cf. *The Poverty of Historicism*, New York, 1964, p. 160.) In each of these definitions by opponents or adherents of historicism, one straightaway finds oneself in a perspective that is foreign to historicism qua philosophical theory; and the critics leave historicized historicism virtually unscathed. What Althusser calls "essence" presents itself within time as no more than an event; but what is an event for one person later becomes a necessity for another and is transformed into an essence when it is interiorized. This mechanism of "valorization," which is part of political theory, is absent from the analysis of historicism qua abstract philosophy. Thus the critique loses its force.

was not this that created the objective conditions for the comparison, since it existed, for that matter, in 1880 or 1900; it was often the same service that in London was analyzing dispatches from Russia, Turkey, Persia, Egypt, and Morocco (around 1904-1906), but was it able to rise to a level of generalization?[10] The two partners had to await the coming of the night (the end of the imperialist era) in order that they might see the rising of the owl of Minerva.

It was after the obtaining of political independence, the coming to power of a provincial petite bourgeoisie, the appearance of an "unattached" Arab intelligentsia of Palestinian origin whose literary production, published in Beirut, were disseminated throughout the Arab world, that the conditions were realized for the emergence of a "second-degree" awareness; that is, the Arabs became aware of their thinking as ideological thinking. A general frame of reference was achieved that at once struck a fatal blow at provincialism, the objective basis of first-degree thinking.

By making successive generalizations and by referring all questions back to one central fact—the failure of all the Arabs in one and the same attempt at liberation—a new formulation of the innovators' original problematic was arrived at.

——What is the most comprehensive definition of imperialism? Is it one of the following elements: political domination, economic exploitation, diplomatic pressure? Or the conjunction of all three? Or must one go even further and state that a hegemonic situation is one in which a single agent makes choices for everyone at all levels, from politics to behavior?

——What is the content of revolution? A rearrangement of the distribution of power, the construction of a national economy, the generalization of technical culture? Can it be better viewed as the liberation of society and the individual

10. One of the negative results of the change in perspective that has occurred in recent colonial history is that the directing center is no longer clearly visible. A certain pointillism results. The reader can find examples in R. Robinson and J. Gallagher, *Africa and the Victorians* (New York, 1968).

from all preconceived limitations (past or future) to the point where the revolutionary society can foresee the actions of its competitors and thus in advance deprive them of their efficacy?

——What is the secret of an underdeveloped society? Above and beyond the lack of technology, the ubiquitous past, and the vanishing future, what is it in such a society that makes words empty or demagogic? Is not the fundamental contradiction the one that exists between an unstable structure (which by its very movement changes the meaning of words and actions) and an ideology of the absolute (God, Democracy, Independence)? In the last analysis, is not the secret of an underdeveloped country the unconscious will on the part of the elite to preserve its absolute at the cost of living individuals, rather than to save the living at the cost of the absolute?[11]

It is easy to see that behind this questioning lies a concept of history as the sole reality. Secularization, the liberation of thought, democratization, development—all these notions and the political choices that can proceed from them are lumped together in an inclusive historicism. This reaction was not confined only to a few individuals. The rethinking that took place after the Arab *Nahda*—a rethinking that has been called the Second *Nahda*[12]—is perhpas the real beginning of a truly adult thought that is wary of its own tendencies and for the first time unfolds outside tradition, in the sense that it does not regard its backwardness as a virtue. What makes it interesting for outsiders is that at a higher level and within the framework of Marxism it again confronts the general problems mentioned in the preceding section. The Second *Nahda* reveals the poverty of Arab Marxism qua ideology, but it

11. For more details, see the preface to the Arabic edition of *L'Idéologie arabe contemporaine* (Beirut, 1970).
12. The phrase takes up the title of a book by Jon Kimche, *The Second Arab Awakening* (New York, 1970); it was used by several participants in a symposium at the Catholic University of Louvain on the contemporary Arab world (November 1970).

enriches Marxist thought. Its experience throws light on the processes by means of which ideologies are propagated.

A SECOND *NAHDA*

Strictly speaking, this began around the years 1963-1965. It arose in the context of an enquiry into the structure of those "progressive" Arab countries in which anticapitalism and anti-imperialism coexisted with an Islamic ideology. It was also nourished by discussions on the formation, psychology, and choices of the chatoyant class whose existence has never ceased to torment socialist thinkers: the petite bourgeoisie.[13] A considerable number of Marxists, who found themselves in agreement with the political choices of these regimes but in utter disagreement with their ideological affiliations, were obliged to confront the complex problem whether the regimes could be inwardly transformed. The knot of contradictions seemed to exist at the ideological level. Well and good. How was it to be united? Some saw in it only the reflection of a class-oriented polity, itself conditioned by insurmountable difficulties in the sphere of economic development; they agreed upon a tactic of pitting class against class and underplayed the national aspect of the anti-imperialist struggle, thus laying themselves open to the fatal accusation that they were playing the enemy's game. Others concentrated their energies on the ideological debate, maintaining on the contrary that class-oriented reductionism (in the actual conditions of the Arab world) was a flight from ideological confrontation that could only result, as in the past, in the

13. See the readings selected by A. Abdel Malek, *La Pensée politique arabe contemporaine* (Paris, 1970). Also Iliās Murquṣ, *Al-Marksiyya wa al-masʾala al-quawmiyya* (Marxism and the National Question), *Al-Marksiyya wa ash-sharq* (Marxism and the East) (Beirut, 1970); Muḥ. Kiᶜhli, *Hawl al-nidhām ar-raʾ smālī fī Lubnān* (On the Capitalist System in Lebanon) (Beirut, 1967); A. Abdel Malek, *Egypt: Military Society: The Army Regime, the Left, and Social Change Under Nasser* (New York); Mahmound Hussein, *La Lutte des classes en Egypte de 1945 à 1970)* (Paris, 1970).

perpetuation of the traditionalist illusion and a preparing of the way for even deadlier regressions. The first group, armed with economic data, showed that the ruling class (whatever social definition of this class one gives), helped by the economic penury, would be as desperate as was the classical nineteenth-century bourgeoisie to defend its acquisitions, even when this meant going against the national interest. The second group, arguing the situation of the Arab countries in the world market, emphasized that the petite bourgeoisie would inevitably deepen its anti-imperialist attitudes and opt for socialism, providing a vigorous ideological campaign was conducted. The age of the petite bourgeoisie was still far from being over, and to concentrate on the ideological struggle, or, more exactly, to give an ideological slant to the political struggle, was actually to repudiate a verbal adventurism that overestimated the freedom of action of the local bureaucracy, when in fact imperialism made it practically impossible for this bureaucracy to swing over into the antinationalist camp and for the other classes to achieve their political or organizational independence. An old debate, no doubt, but here it applied to a real situation.

It became yet more intense after 1967. New periodicals and publishers specialized in material (consisting of both theoretical discussion and analysis of particular cases) that fueled the debate.[14] We will not concern ourselves with the factual side of this debate, but with the way in which it intensifies (on the methodical level) the issues of historicism adumbrated in the preceding pages.

Like all observers, the Arabs were impressed by the essentially political, and therefore social, character of the 1967 defeat.[15] All at once the debate centered on the reasons

14. E.g., in Beirut, the review *Dirāsāt ʿArabiyya* (Arab Studies) published by Dar aṭ-Ṭalīʿa (Avant-garde), which existed before 1967; the review *Mawāqif* (Standpoints), and the publishing house Dar al-Haqiqa (Truth), which was founded at a later date.
15. See Nadim Al-Baitar, *Min al-Naksa ilā ath-Thawra* (From Relapse—tactical retreat—to Revolution) (1968), which summarizes

and modalities of the backwardness of ideology in relation to
the social structure and, still more important, in relation to
the technological and economic substructure. If this was
debated mainly among Arab Marxists, it was because the
problem seemed especially formidable to those who had
failed to confront it for so many years. (They had berated
those who *had* been preoccupied with it for being impenitent
idealists.) The Western evolutionists and liberals have always
thought that Westernization begins in the foreign schools,
that tradition was the exact measure of delay in the diffusion
of democratic-liberal ideology.[16] The action entered by the
participants in this debate against Arab society and against
the ruling class was at the same time a trial of Arab Marxism,
itself the result of a deviation from Marxist method. Whence
a natural recourse to the basic attitude of Lenin, who was the
first to dare to distinguish Marxism qua method of analysis
from Marxism qua social phenomenon, and who refused to
act as if all societies since Marx had to live in a perpetual
present. Tirelessly to repeat Marx is to become the object, and
solely the object, of history and no longer to master its
practice; it was a matter, therefore, of interiorizing the
implicit system on the basis of which Marx criticized his time.
However, can this requirement be met, or is one condemned,
if one is unwilling to embark on the hazardous and unrealizable quest for a Logos in its natural state, to keep it as a
formal axiom?

As a matter of fact, the progressive Arab ideologists

---

most of the arguments used in the issues of *Dirāsāt ʿArabiyya.*
Bernard Lewis, who (in *Foreign Affairs,* vol. III [1968]) believes he
has detected an element of unrealism in the fact that the 1948 defeat
is called a *nakba* (catastrophe) and the far greater defeat of 1967 a
naksa (relapse), shows that he has failed to grasp the reality of the
Second *Nahda.*
16. On this specific point, studies on Westernization misplace and
obfuscate the problem with a methodological unilateralism. A very
revealing example is Nadav Safran's book, *Egypt in Search of a
Political Community* (Cambridge, Mass., 1961), in which, owing to
preconceptions, many just observations are lost in a superficial
conclusion.

hereabouts are recovering the path of historicism: just as Marx provides them with an analytical handbook of the bourgeoisie, so does Lenin epitomize for them the period of the imperialist hegemony and Mao Tse-tung epitomize the national democratic revolution. The belief that one can take up history at the point where these practitioners found it— i.e., before they gave it an irreversible direction—is a fatal illusion, which in the long run results in a capitulation to the forces of hegemony and its dialectical opposite, tradition. Reviewing all the inappropriate actions of the past, one is forced to concede the futility of all the (Stoic) illusions concerning the freedom of men who are dominated. Everything depends, to be sure, on the irreducible lapse of time that separates what one says from what happens. To believe on principle in this freedom is to subscribe to eclecticism and to follow blindly after events that do not wait for us; whereas to believe in the ineluctability of an already given course (and if one lays emphasis here upon the diversity of modalities of application, one is mostly encouraging the illusion of liberty) is to give oneself a chance of effectively impinging upon social evolution: it is historicism in action. We have to choose between abandoning history to the chance play of commerce and war or unifying it with a deliberate universalism.[17]

RECURRENCES OF TRADITION

The critique made by the progressive Arab ideologists of the thinkers who preceded them was to bear on three fundamental points: the persistence of tradition; the concept of

17. Between an eclecticism without inner logic and an historicism without apparent liberty, it will be said that there is room for a methodic adoption of scientificity, as L. Althusser maintains. If he hits the mark on several occasions (*Reading Capital, op. cit.*, p. II, chs. 4 and 5) when he wishes to preserve the autonomy of scientific practice—this point remains largely theoretical in the context of the Third World—he neglects the autonomy of political practice, which for the Third World intellectual is of the essence. Political practice imposes historicism as a self-evident necessity, a "natural ideology."

politics; and the perpetual, multilevelled "ideologization" of thought.

How is it that tradition, continually reinterpreted and revalued, has lost nothing of its influence while passing (by way of the colonial era) from the age of the foreign aristocracy to the reign of the petite bourgeoisie? Simplified Marxism, like colonial evolutionism, had encouraged belief in the axiom, "Overthrow the base and everything will disintegrate." In practice this was everywhere shown to be illusory. Doubtless there exists no one tradition (no one Islam), and, if we are to make the necessary distinctions, we have no alternative but to pursue extended researches in the area of religious sociology. These alone might tell us whether the Islam of such and such a social group at such and such a time was a religion, a social ethic, or simply a badge of membership. Doubtless, the philological or structural analysis of the normative Islam tells us nothing about the mechanism of its social effectiveness. But time presses and we must take a stand. By what is contemporary Islamic ideology characterized? The following traits can be singled out:

——A nationalist tendency; that is, one that presents the recent past as an undeserved decadence and the future as a promise that sooner or later will be fulfilled.

——An anticapitalism that is conceived chiefly as a token of separation from the West.

——An egalitarian statism that consolidates communal unity (itself an indispensable condition of the promised renaissance).

——An intrinsic and irreducible utopianism.

This is the Islam that explicitly or implicitly sustains the greater part of the Arab intelligentsia, and it permeates the declarations of the most prestigious political figures. However, beyond these particular aspects, which certainly deserve to be examined, there remains another and fundamental aspect that (on the evidence) goes often unperceived: this is faith in the unknowable *(ghayb)*. This point should no longer be passed over in silence.

Ṣadīq Jalāl al-ʿAdhm takes up the challenge. Returning to the texts of lectures delivered before 1967, whose pertinency and cogency have since become all the more apparent, he has written a book that entirely conforms with the exigencies of rational analysis.[18] How does he go about his task? He contents himself with comparing what an educated Muslim of today must believe as a Muslim with what he has learned since his first years at secondary school on the subject of Newtonian physics; the inevitable consequence—a scandalous split that inheres in the Muslim's heart and mind—is thus made glaringly apparent. He describes, precisely and in detail, the intellectual anguish that results, the emptiness of a widespread attitude of compromise that pervades the entire society and extends from the theoretical domain of Islam's relations with modern science to the interdenominational entente in Lebanon. Taking his analysis further, he shows (in the most striking part of his book, a brilliant study of the role of Iblīs in Muslim eschatology) that not even the religious Muslim who is versed in Greek tragedy and the writings of Kierkegaard can bridge this intrinsic fissure of consciousness.[19]

Today faith must be heroic or nothing. Whatever his personal choice, the author plainly thinks that a renewal of faith forms part of the total renewal of society, while the existing conformism is the symbol of general stagnation.

Doubtless this is an attitude with a long history,[20] but

18. His book is called *Naqd al-Fikr ad-dīnī* (A Critique of the Religious Mind), 2nd ed. (Beirut, 1970); it includes the proceedings of the action entered against the author by the attorney general on behalf of the Islamic associations of Lebanon.
19. Quoting beautiful passages from al-Hallāj, *Tawāsin,* and from ʿIzz ad-Dīn al-Maqdisī, *Taflīs Iblīs* (Cairo, 1906), he shows that Iblīs (Satan) has simply played the role eternally assigned to him in the cosmic drama; he must therefore be rehabilitated since he obeys the Law of the world rather than a circumstantial order. Thus traditional faith becomes problematic.
20. See M. Mhadi's observations, in "Remarks on the Theologus Autodidactus of Ibn al-Nafis" *(SI,* XXXI, pp. 197-209), on the indirect manner in which the classical Muslim savants demonstrated the bankruptcy of theology.

conditions have never been so favorable for an interiorization
of these antinomies. The author indicts all socialists, whether
Marxist or not, and even liberals, with having forgotten that
in Europe a free-thinking movement, atheist or deist, preceded the socialist crusade, and that the liberation of the mind
and the individual must logically precede the liberation of
society. To neglect this precondition or to dismiss it as
yesterday's achievement is to do a great disservice to
everyone.[21]

Ṣadīq al-ʿAdhm, however, does not transcend the framework of liberalism. Merely to describe the contradictions of
Islamic consciousness tells us nothing about the real historical
problem: the mechanisms that make possible the recurrence
of Islamic ideology.

Here we meet with the question of local involution.[22]
Methodic studies on the colonial period in the Arab countries
are still not numerous, but historians are becoming increasingly aware of the dialectical connection between involution
and imperialist hegemony. Anwar Abdel Malek,[23] for example, takes up Muḥammad ʿAbduh's analysis of *salafiyya* (or
fundamentalism, according to his terminology). Rejecting
any structuralist parti pris and adopting an exclusively
historiographical point of view, he structures his book in
such a way that ʿAbduh emerges as the simple product of
Lord Cromer's cultural policy. Some will consider the mon-
tage a little too rapid, the demonstration too abrupt, but
Abdel Malek is less interested in ʿAbduh's ideas, in their
internal arrangement, than in the manner of their social
propagation, and many facts corroborate his intuitions about

21. In this perspective, the Islamic tolerance that depends on social
conformity and juridicial literalism is no longer considered a positive
asset. *Taqiyya* (mental reservation) and the double truth become
negative motifs of our past. The author doubtless intended his trial
to be exemplary.
22. The idea of involution has been felicitously used by Clifford
Geertz in his works on Indonesia. Remaining on the socioeconomic
level, however, he does no more than illustrate Engels' theses on
Ireland.
23. *Idéologie et renaissance nationale: l'Egypte moderne* (Paris,
1969), chs. 10 and 11.

this. First, the question of India, where Cromer made his apprenticeship: why do we find a wave of traditionalism on the subcontinent and nothing comparable in China, whose past was even more august? Next, in the Arab sphere: why the rapid expansion of Wahhābism, Mahdism, and the *Sanūsiiyya* movement, in proportion as foreign pressure became more intense? It would seem to be established (although strictly speaking this is a hypothesis) that we can no longer ignore the dialectical connection between an overthrow of the base and the "regressive" ideological response that accompanies it. As we have seen for so many years in the Arab countries, Marxism has been spellbound by liberal linear evolutionism, and it has not been able to play any role in the elucidation of the Arab past, which perhaps for the most part consists of a succession of regressive reactions. This deficiency doubtless explains many of its failures and its lack of resolve. For this reason, today's Marxist resurgence is characterized chiefly by an abandonment of these habits of thought.

The perspectives revealed by a re-examination of tradition by no means end here.

On the level of political practice, the colonial period was one of applied liberalism, against which tradition took a stand; national liberalism could be nothing if not the natural justification and maintenance of the status quo. Revolutionary action theoretically amounts to a rectification of ideological backwardness by a relative justification of both tradition and liberalism.

This rectification may be reduced to the following postulate: the transition from a given social structure to another is obligatory, and every reactualization of the past is illusory. The therapeutic value of such a reactualization derives solely from the fact that it is consciously assumed. The hypothesis of a unified history is common to the liberal and to the revolutionary, but only the latter embodies and finally verifies it. The historicism we are leading up to, one that is in many respects instrumental, is not the passive acceptance of any past whatsoever and above all not the acceptance of one's own national past (organicist conservatism, which is never entirely sincere); rather, it is the voluntary choice of realizing the unity of historical meaning by the reappropriation of a selective past. This choice is motivated by pragmatic considerations, perhaps by modesty, above all by nationalism in the most natural sense of the word: the will to gain the respect of others by the shortest possible route. In this perspective we see clearly that it is not the moderate liberal who is being realistic, for he chooses to believe in the improbable equality of nations. Rather, it is the radical nationalist who is the realist; provided that he affirms his existence, he cares little if he loses his essence (his authenticity).

Praxis is therefore historicism in action. And it should come as no surprise that all antihistoricism takes on an anti-praxis value. An abstract universalism, expressing itself in economism, anthropology, or structuralism, knows nothing of involution and consequently takes no account of hegemony. Even at the level of history, an analogous result may be arrived at if one works with monad-like societies that are closed in upon themselves and placed upon the same plane at points unequally distant from an identical starting or finishing line; this was the perspective of evolutionism. Escapes toward the infra- or the suprahistoric are to be found within Marxism itself, and they tend to perpetuate ideological retardation by formally denying it. Hence the Third World intelligentsia's condemnations of cultural imperialism. Sometimes people are puzzled by the ill-treatment meted out to the old liberal paternalism, to Marxist Europeocentrism, and to structuralist antiracism (Lévi-Strauss). This is because they are unwilling to see how these can form part of the same hegemonic system.

Once again we arrive at the reciprocal determination of the four concepts: hegemony, involution, praxis, and historicism;[24] this reflection is not, properly speaking, a rereading

24. One sees straightaway that the four concepts and their formal structure can be transposed into the language of psychoanalysis. This explains the fascination of the latter for Third World intellec-

of Marx—that, after all that has happened in the world since the writing of *Capital*, would be a meaningless task. Rather, it enriches, deepens, and reopens discussion of ideas that form an important part of contemporary Western culture.

THE CONCEPT OF POLITICS

In the absence of a guideline (historicist consciousness), everything becomes subject to evolution and hence the victim of retardation. Eclecticism perpetuates ideological backwardness, the symbol of domination that is in the process of being consolidated; conversely, hegemony perpetuates eclecticism by creating backwardness. And Marxism by no means escapes from this law: once the algebra of revolution, it becomes the arithmetic of stagnation.

In answer to the question, To what, in a dominated society, is eclecticism attributable? one tends increasingly to reply: To the elite's lack of homogeneity. To reach this conclusion, we have had to break (on this point also) with a certain traditional analysis that answered the challenge of the "elitist" schools by simply denying the autonomy of politics. This economically inspired analysis proved utterly incapable of seeing the colonial or imperialist phenomenon in its deepest signification. Putting all societies on the same level, though at

---

tuals; for psychoanalysis, speaking to them individually, seems to be more propitious for literary creation. In this respect the material published by the review *Mawāqif* is symptomatic. In Abdelkebir Khatibi's novel *La Mémoire totouée* (Paris, 1971) the author, describing his personal strivings to achieve decolonization, consciously plays on the two registers, individual and collective. Each conceptual critique of psychoanalysis therefore carries little weight, for it is immediately translated into the language of psychoanalysis. Only practice would demonstrate that the evidence of experience is illusory, that reduction of the sociohistoric structure to that of analyzed personal experience opens the way to eclectic formalism, and that the form that derives from it is aesthetically incomplete (poetry turns into lyricism, drama becomes an elegiac duet, and the novel becomes a long short story). It can be no more than a moment, albeit in some respects a captivating moment, of human sensibility in its path toward objectivity, prose, historicity.

different positions; denying the persistent effectivity of the
national past, of tradition, and of polity as government of
man; and forgetting that the definition of *homo politicus* as
rational man is a relatively recent conquest; it presupposed
that the determinations between economy, society, and
typical polity are always normal, mediate, and direct.[25]
Starting with a generalization, it ended in abstraction. In the
hour of danger a certain twentieth-century European liberalism opted for a racially inspired otherness; in answer, this
simplified Marxism returned to the facile optimism of nineteenth-century positivism. Every group in power saw itself
credited with the totality of the attributes of the classical
bourgeoisie; its policies could therefore be precisely foreseen,
just as it was anticipated that a working class, wherever it
might be, would normally do what was expected of it.[26]
However, experience shows that a military government does
not behave as if it were the embodiment of the petite
bourgeoisie, and the latter does not show the same resource-
fulness as the English bourgeoisie. Preoccupied with tireless
repetition of the same diatribes against a political order that
manifestly continues to change—but not in the anticipated
direction—the Arab Marxists left it to the English-speaking
political scientists to disclose real problems and stumbling
blocks.

By very different means, and by concentrating on three
specific areas—namely, the structure and formation of the

25. This analysis follows with apparent logic from Marx's axiom
that vis-à-vis capitalism all precapitalist societies are equally power-
less. Here one sees that, when trying to diagnose the problems of
the Third World, the unpardonable error is to pass Lenin over: one
falls inevitably into liberalism.
26. One may be tempted to generalize this critique and say that
abstraction is part and parcel of all applied historicism. Let it be
noted, however, that the instance under discussion is a borderline
one, which would be difficult to parallel. In the second place,
eclecticism, which stems from a hyperpositivism, does not escape
from abstraction either. And this is a danger lying in wait for all
"politics," even when it parades the latest findings of opinion polls.

political elite, the mechanism of political practice, and political "culture"—a degree of rationality was introduced into the study of what had hitherto been regarded as belonging strictly to the domain of psychological impressionism: popular passivity, corruption, cynicism.[27] Conceding a fault of method in the mixture of facile empiricism and excessive theoretical formalization by which it is characterized, and admitting the pragmatism of conclusions that are always oriented toward the possible emergence of a positive nationalism and a stable structure, it remains nonetheless true that this approach has challenged the very concept of politics for the first time and in an indirect manner. Political rationality begins to be separated from economic utilitarianism; the emergence of the elite is no longer a matter of strict class determinism but is influenced by culture and history. Let us note in passing that in the United States this change of perspective is due partly to a return in force, through Max Weber and German historicism in general, of historicist methodology. The Arab intelligentsia of the left, rediscovering historicism in its own manner, has been brought around to consider the same problems, though in a more theoretical framework.

Iliās Murquṣ, in his polemic directed at a group of Palestinian revolutionaries,[28] advances three theses against his adversaries. Forcibly denying the direct determination of politics by economy, he naturally makes use of the Lenin of *What Is to Be Done?* against this "economism." In the second place, and as a consequence, he denies the equation of petite

27. Because the countries in question are closed to them, American political science specialists who are concerned with the Middle East regard themselves as lagging behind their colleagues working on Latin America and Southeast Asia. As far as the points raised in the text the most suggestive books, many errors of detail notwithstanding, are: John Waterbury, *Commander of the Faithful* (New York, 1970); and Marvin Zonis, *The Political Elite of Iran* (Princeton, 1971).

28. *ʿAfwiyyat al-Nadhariyya fī al-ʿAmal al-Fidāʾī* (Spontaneism in the Theory of the Palestinian Resistance), vol. I (Dar al-Haqiqa, 1970).

bourgeoisie with ruling group, and in this connection returns
several times to the logical error that consists of directly
drawing a particular abstract conclusion from a general law
and then presenting this conclusion as an observed reality. In
the third place, he denies that the problematic of class can
absorb, or transcend, the national problematic (at least in the
immediate future). This is the most important point, and it
bears essentially on a problem of fact; upon it depends all
effective political action. Murquṣ maintains that his position
amounts to a full realization of that reality which is imperialist hegemony. If a group wants a chance of success, it must
conceive of and put into practice a "response" that is the fruit
of an analysis of the total world situation, and this response
can only be the historical project of national liberation.
Beyond the appeal of Lenin, what we find in this writer is
the revenge of historical depth upon the synchronistic analysis of the relations between social groups. In his view it is not
the evolution of the export trade of the Arab countries,
repercussing on one or more groups, that will permit us to
understand the present polities of these countries and hence
to determine, by means of elementary formal reversal, other
and more revolutionary polities; the cause should rather be
sought in the European decision of 1840[29] and its uninterrupted consequences. Murquṣ redisovers historical depth in
everyday political practice; he seeks his references in Lenin
and, having found them, looks no further. But we may extend
his thinking in conjunction with the results of the English
and American political science alluded to above.

It is interesting to note that Arab "economism" develops in
certain specific conditions in reaction to evolutionist Marxism
(of the traditional Communist parties). Thus the negation of
history and politics answers to a negation of another kind,
and we truly discover Lenin when we are concerned to criticize both of them at the same time. We often make our
first real reading of an author, not when we would simply

29. This was England's decision to stop Mohammed Ali's offensive
against the Ottoman Sultan.

desire to do so, but when conditions demand it. The logic of Leninism is reincarnated once again, and theoretical disputes become life-and-death problems.

The rediscovery, through Lenin, of the autonomy of politics confronts us immediately with formidable questions. Is it an accident that this autonomy was first affirmed in countries with a strong historicist tradition, whatever use was subsequently made of it? Is it accidental that it was again taken up and analyzed by A. Gramsci in the context of Machiavelli, to whom he returned after a long detour by way of the German school of history, Bismarck, Croce? Cannot the Arabs of today, by taking the same long detour, encounter it in the form expressed or symbolized by the trio Ibn Bāja—Ibn Khaldūn—Ibn Taimiyya? In all parts of the world where manipulation of men has for centuries supplanted administration of things, politics will not be easily assimilated with economics.

If ever there were intellectuals who ought not to have let themselves be caught in the false antinomy of class/elite, it was the Arab intellectuals, who daily lived beneath the weight of the past and who knew by experience the double determination of society and history. It is an illusion to postulate the direct determination of the elite by class, and it is an abusive generalization to affirm the homogeneity of the elite and its absolute independence. A more concrete and complex model would permit us to preserve the autonomy of politics, but it would do so in a global setting. It would show the abstract nature of both liberal evolutionism, of which Marxist "economism" is merely a variant, and the conservative essentialism that threatens to rise again from its ashes if the thesis of an autonomous elite is pushed too far. The Arab revolutionary intelligentsia can profit greatly from Gramsci's remarks, provided that it takes care to reinterpret them in the context of the Arab political tradition.[30]

30. It is revealing that the first translation of this author should have appeared in 1969: *Al-Amīr al-Hadīth* (The Modern Prince), trans. Zahī Sharfān and Anīs Shāmī (Dar aṭ-Ṭalīʿa).

In the long run, this debate will enable us to shed some light upon the historical conditions that gave birth to elitism itself. In what circumstances is its methodology adequate to its object, and can it escape from its ideological function as a weapon against class analysis? (This has hitherto been its role in the United States.)

DOUBLE IDEOLOGIZATION

Sectional involution and the autonomy of the elite—two aspects of the same phenomenon of domination that are completed by a third: the double ideologization of ideologies. Logomachy *(kalāmulujiya,* as Murquṣ says) is first a social fact.

Ideology (in the primary sense) that is directly produced by culture is intrinsically inadequate, and will always remain so. The ideology or ideologies that come from outside gradually take shape at the hands of those who adopt them. By what mechanisms? Lenin said that the working class always got its Marxism from outside; we still have to specify which working class and which society. Gramsci pondered the role of intellectuals for a working class whose members still have a Ptolemaic conception of the world.[31] The Arab ideologists are encountering this problem in an infinitely more complicated situation.

The elite's autonomy confers on it a capacity for infinite subdivision, and creates an increasing need for distinguishing signs: these are the ideologies in the banal sense of the word,

31. "A class, certain strata of which still have a Ptolemaic conception of the world, may nevertheless figure in an advanced socio-economic situation; ideologically backward . . . , these strata are nevertheless very advanced from the practical viewpoint, that is, from the viewpoint of economic and political function. If the task of the intellectuals is to determine and organize moral and cultural reform—that is, to make culture and political practice coincide—it is evident that crystallized intellectuals are conservatives and reactionaries." *(Oeuvres choisies, op. cit.,* pp. 158-159.) Here one clearly sees where praxis is "rectification."

imported as readily as new fashions in clothes. Marxism with
all its nuances is no exception to the rule. One could therefore
make a study of the introduction and propagation of this
token Marxism, and indeed there are Marxists, witnesses to
the development of recognized parties that were as independent of society as any other political elite, who have recently
undertaken to do so.

For the moment let me defer comment on two aspects of
this Marxism: its degree of assimilation (Arabization) and its
degree of dogmatism; let me say only that they point in
opposite directions and that both depend on the evolution of
society as a whole. Assimilation cannot take place, and
dogmatism cannot be diluted, unless method finds its object;
that is, unless society permits the trying out of models
inscribed upon consciousness.[32]

The striking thing about the short history of Arab Marxism
is that it has passed through the three well-known stages:
populist Marxism, which has seen its effects diluted in the
larger current of Islamic utopianism; legal Marxism, into
which the ideology of the parties, born under the sign of
Leninism, was transformed; and economic Marxism, which
rapidly transforms itself into "spontaneism." Why have we
passed through this identical experience of ideological differentiation? Even as an importation, Marxism should not
necessarily have reproduced itself in all its nuances; so it is by

32. In this connection, it is perhaps necessary to distinguish two
types of dogmatism, pre- and post-revolutionary, for between the
two exists a period of positive "revision" when society is revolutionized. We are referring to Engels' dogmatism, not to Stalin's. In
both, however, the concept of totality is central, as it is in all
historicist thought; it is against this concept that Althusser's and,
before him, Karl Popper's critiques are directed. On a strictly
theoretical level the debate is issueless and perhaps objectless; it is at
the level of political practice that it must be settled. Popper recognizes, moreover, that historicism and activism are indissolubly
linked. If one does not place the distinction between dominant and
dominated society at the center of one's thinking, one may in point
of fact conclude that the concept of totality is inimical both to
science and to liberty.

reflecting on this similarity of development, by verifying the Leninist hypotheses, that certain Arab intellectuals are redis-covering historicism—even at the ideological level. On what basis, indeed, does Iliās Murquṣ, who declares himself a Marxist-Leninist, make his case against "economism" or liberal Western Marxism? We have already said that his analysis of "spontaneism" leads to the necessity for the formulation of a national historical project. According to him, this is nothing other than the project of Arab unity. Economic Marxists ("spontaneists") and legal Marxists (lib-erals) actually repudiate this project; their analysis, not being founded on history, does not envision it as being inscribed in the real, does not apprehend it as the necessary outcome of the imperialist hegemony.[33] To become aware of the histori-cal goal of imperialism since 1840 is ipso facto to make unity an exigency of reality. From the moment that the historical dimension enters the analysis, the goal of unity is discern-ible.[34] The future of a given ideology is not assured unless it offers the possibility of concretizing the frustrated hopes of a community. It was by reflecting on the accumulated back-wardness of Russian society—its unequal development within the framework of world capitalism—that the secret of an uninterrupted revolution was revealed; similarly, it is by becoming aware of all the obstacles on the road to unity that we shall give modern Arab history its meaning and weight; so, too, shall we find the real significance of the imperialist hegemony and the revolutionary "response's" real prospect of success. Finding Arab unity at the end of the argument, we can work our way back through its various stages: unity, an autonomous elite, dislocation of society, hegemony. It is the

33. Cf. the scattered remarks on the colonial policy of the Second International in Iliās Murquṣ' book, *Al-Marksiya wa ash-sharq* (Marxism and the East) (Dar aṭ-Ṭalīʿa, 1968).
34. Although sharing the same historicist concern, A. Abdel Malek, who remains faithful to the inspiration of the *Wafd*, does not reach the same conclusion. One would have to corroborate this with a more thorough investigation than is attempted here, but it seems that on this point Iliās Murquṣ' analysis is the more rigorous.

same conceptual system reappearing at several levels; behind it the historicist frame of reference can always be discerned. Whatever path we follow, we shall inevitably reach this common ground.

In the last analysis, it is a historicization of Marxism that we are discussing. Historicist Marxism seems to be the only Marxism capable of apprehending the entire spectrum of experiential reality; consequently, it is the only Marxism that can effectively act on that reality. The rational necessity of its present advent is a sign that a profound change has taken place. For the first time Arab society is interiorizing historicity in a positive manner, not negatively, as it has so often done in the past under the cover of mysticism. If this historicization continues to be merely theoretical, however, it will do nothing to modify the eclecticism of the elite, whose social significance we have already discussed. If there must be a second "true" *Nahda*—which is sometimes described as a dynamization *(tathwīr)* of Arab thought—this Marxism must seek to apply itself in searching studies of the elite, of the economic base regarded as a part of the world system, and of the mechanism of ideologization. At each stage, the analysis of synchronous relations should be subordinated to genetic filiation, for it was a shallow structuralism (a new expression of liberal evolutionism) that gave birth to such utterly abstract notions as national capitalism, national bourgeoisie, and national democracy. The concretization of this historicist Marxism is the culmination of a long ideological struggle to give Arab society a complete and convincing image of its present and its past.

By this means society will be modernized, the elite will be integrated with society, and ideology will be concretized; the road to political legitimacy is thus laid out. At the same time a more or less forgotten meaning of praxis will be found again: the "realization" by political action of a semantic system, this in turn supporting political aims. When such a Marxism becomes the inner logic of what Arab society has to say of itself, the latter will have assimilated, by way of ideological struggle, the definitive acquisitions of utilitarianism, liberalism, historicism.[35] A "political Logos" will have been created that alone will permit the real application of the political program that has been talked about for so long: agrarian reform, democracy, national independence.

But if it is a question only of the historicization of thought, this can be carried out in any system whatever, even (it will be said) in theology. H. A. R. Gibb invited the ʿulamā to the practice of history, and he was not listened to. In fact, neither the *shaykhs* nor the liberals can historicize their thought,[36] because the former refuse to acknowledge backwardness and the latter refuse to acknowledge the ineluctable inequalities of national development. They will not do so until society has assimilated historicism through the intense ideological struggle of the Marxists. After all, Ṣadīq al-ʿAdhm is perhaps working, without exactly desiring it, for the renewal of religious thought.

HISTORICISM AND REALISM

Has this historicism in action, which has been rediscovered by the revolutionary Arab intelligentsia, any signification other than a local one?

As it has emerged in the preceding analyses, historicism (contrary to what is often believed) is the most positive form of universalism. All shades of positivist thought, liberal or

35. A. Gramsci writes: "The philosophy of praxis is 'absolute historicism'; it is thought that becomes absolutely mundane and terrestrial, an absolute humanism of history." (*Oeuvres choisies, op. cit.*, p. 171.) He had previously demonstrated the intellectuals' role in the moral and intellectual reform of classes that are advanced from the practical point of view. The recent experience of the revolutionary Arab intelligentsia would appear to be an illustration of this analysis. 36. An example of this incapacity on the part of the *shaykh* is Muḥ. al Bahi's *Al-Fikr al-Islāmī al-Hadīth wa ṣilatuhu bi al-Istiʿmār al-Gharbī* (Modern Islamic Thought and Its Relation to Western Imperialism), 5th ed. (Beirut, 1970); and on the part of the liberal, Hasan Saʿb, *Tahdīth al-Fikr al-ʿArabī* (Modernization of the Arab Mentality) (Beirut, 1970). The two books are nonetheless interesting.

Marxist, take note of the universalism brought about by technology and world commerce and fail to see involutions (inequalities of development between societies and within the same society); whence an incapacity to come to terms with the forces of reaction, be they romantic or nationalistic.[37] In this frame of reference, historicism is reduced to the philosophy of the practice of history, and ought perhaps to be called "historism" once and for all; a theory of passivity, it justifies folkloric differences in paths of development and prepares the ground for that total otherness which relegates unity to the infrahistorical (the infancy of societies, of the individual, or of the mind), or projects it outward into extra-terrestrial dreams (stellar colonization and cosmic death).

The other historicism emerges at the level of political practice when the elite makes a definite ideological choice: that of resolving the dichotomy between ideology and structure. It is by reflecting on the failure of liberalism, seemingly accepted or passively submitted to by historism and often symbolized by great national catastrophes—Jena, Novara, Port Arthur, etc.—that the goal is fixed: abstracted by the ideologist, the model of what has proved effective elsewhere is to be revived and reconcretized. This is the time when the man of praxis considers he has but one choice: that of making happen what has happened before (due allowance made for differing circumstances). Folkloric differences will doubtless continue (language, culinary tradition, music, song, etc.), but will hardly influence the national project. By reincarnating the model, the man of praxis objectivizes historicism: the unitary path of historical development, the

37. English and American cultural analysis, influenced by the German experience, traditionally links romanticism, historicism, and nationalism. This is not so with French traditional analysis (with the exception of the all-too-short studies of Eric Weil); the result is a restriction of the meaning of both historicism and romanticism. See R. Girardet, "Autour de l'idéologie nationaliste" *(Revue française de science politique* [Paris, 1965], pp. 423-445); H. Lefebvre, "Le Romantisme révolutionnaire" *(Nouvelle Revue française* [Paris, Oct. 1957], pp. 644-672).

general truth that is given solely in and through history. Of what importance is it that the philosopher of history or the historian of philosphy decides in the abstract: history has no meaning? It is the man of praxis (who is anywhere but in the society of his detractors) that settles the question by adopting an ideology aiming at universality, leaving to the philosophers only the task of interpreting his actions.[38]

Historicism, then, is but another face of realism—the realism that conduces to lasting equilibrium among individuals, groups, and nations. Indeed, is not "reality" a moment in the analytical schema or plan of action through which one must pass?[39]

Nonetheless, many believe that the sole basis for universality is the abstract logic of science. Let us recall that there have been great names in the historicist tradition who have come to exactly the opposite conclusion, and that protestations of astonishment have been hitherto the only response to their remarks.[40] It will be said that all this logic inspired by Hegel—he too was an enemy of Newtonian mechanics—amounts to little more than a game with words. Each is free to think so, on condition that he does not forget there is another game—one that is not entirely innocent. This is the game of the conservatives, Arab or non-Arab, who oppose Marxist historicism with the evidence of mathematical logic while refusing to see that universal agreement at this level of abstraction would do nothing to expose inequalities or to insure against bitterness and revolt. And there is another game, one that consists of searching for man in what lies beyond man, in the laws of dream and rhetoric. The world is a Divine dream and this dream is in the Word. All the mosques, all the caverns, all the caravanserais of the vast

38. This was already true for the propagation of the religions.
39. Many examples are found in the lives of the great revolutionaries. The same is also true of Iliās Murquṣ and the Palestinian conflict.
40. See C. Lichtheim's remarks on Lukács in *Studies in the Philosophy of History* (New York, 1965), p. 174. On Gramsci and his "astonishing" positions, see J. Texier's contribution to the *Philosophes de tous les temps* series (Paris, 1966), p. 77.

world of Islam have reverberated with this feverish affirmation; our science, for centuries, was no more than a striving to render explicit the Divine Name *(Ism)*.[41]

Only one antidote has so far been found for what is the inner demon of every Arab intellectual, and that is historicism. To devaluate historicism is therefore a form of cultural aggression.

APPENDIX: EUROPE AND NON-EUROPE

There came a time when Europe moved out of Europe; making conquest after conquest, it eventually dominated the entire earth. This fact is not new.

How does the hegemony of the last two centuries differ from the hegemonies of the past? At the present time it is impossible to answer this question; it has been possible, however, to make a preliminary step by attempting to reach a general problematic governing the European encounter with non-European peoples. This encounter has taken many forms, all of which should be studied and compared.

Europe began by imposing its arms, God, laws, commerce, and languages upon the non-European peoples. This first form of hegemony, which coincided with a feeling of isolation and impotence (for years the Turks were before the gates of Vienna), entailed no discontinuity with the past—not even with the immediate past. At the same time, the missionaries sent to Asia (but not to Islam) were urging acceptance of their God by roundabout means; the timidity of their approach bespoke a recognition of the power of others. This recognition of the non-European, directly observed for the first time but not yet integrated, receives ideological expression in the relativism of a Montaigne, the tolerance of a Voltaire, the historicism of a Herder.

41. For this central point in the cultural history of the Arabs, see M. Mahdi, "Language and Logic in Classical Islam," in *Logic in Classical Islamic Culture*, ed. G. von Grunebaum (Wiesbaden, 1970), pp. 51-83.

The second form of hegemony, coinciding with the slow development of the industrial revolution, attained its apogee in the mid-nineteenth century. The world was being rounded into final shape, divided among the principal European countries; Asia was said to be sleeping, the East was decadent, Turkey a sick man. The relationship established was the kind in which violence, persuasion, and threats alternated. The world went to school—the school of Europe. It was the age of the Reforms, of Europeanization, of Young Turkey and Young China. But then reaction set in. Europe's message to everyone was: "Do as I do." The reply became: "But who are you?" From that moment to the present the dialogue has not abated. Transforming others, Europe transforms itself; questioned by others, Europe must question itself. The First World War extended this dialectic: the Second World War has given it central importance.

These relations can be studied on different levels: that of exoticism (the East in French and English literature), that of politics (the history of constitutional movements in China or Turkey), or that of economics (the much-debated problem of underdevelopment); the tendency, however, is to prefer the psycho-ideological level. One of the principal reasons for this is that the peoples concerned are now active participants in the debate; since we are all involved, it can no longer be described from outside. That this study is important is self-evident: it permits us to understand the dynamic of the past half-century. And it is not only the past that concerns us, but the present reality of the relations between peoples and nations and of their possible development.

I. The Problem

After a military defeat, a "traditionalist" State finds itself confronted with a series of demands: it must become open to European commerce; in order to encourage such commerce, it must introduce "objective" legislation, that is, a judicial system conforming to European law; and it must guarantee the safety of foreign merchants by reforming its army and its police—these three reforms being considered necessary conditions of civilization. The European soldier, merchant, and diplomat are followed by the military instructor, the legal adviser, and the financier. China, Japan, Turkey, Egypt, Tunisia, Morocco—these countries found themselves, in different degrees, confronted with this situation. At this stage, only the governments of these countries were directly concerned, and they had no alternative but to submit; their sole defense was to temporize. However, the governments had to justify to their peoples the introduction of innovations under evident foreign pressure. Thus they often launched a sort of referendum, while letting it be clearly understood what result they expected (Japan in 1853, Morocco in 1886). The justifications were all of a practical nature; problems were seen in the framework of the old relations of power and force. Nevertheless, these compulsory reforms necessitated a new education; the missionaries, profiting from a new situation, opened schools whose utility soon made itself felt. It was against these developments that reaction set in, for the foundation of traditional society was very quickly imperiled. The opposition pivoted on the old aristocracy, which was frequently pre-eminent in government. The situation was not the same everywhere; the reaction was to be most violent and lasting wherever the aristocracy was defined in cultural terms (*literati* in China, *ᶜulamā* in Islam). The guardian of religious and cultural values, this class was quick to feel itself endangered; it saw clearly that its own interests and those of the State were already beginning to diverge. It embarked upon a systematic attack against the new culture. This is the phase of *cultural nationalism,* which analysts today have difficulty in distinguishing from later forms of nationalism (al-Afghānī's ideology is a case in point), for it is not two nations, two races, or even two religions, that it seeks to confront, but what are in essence two cultures. As it is the fact of contradiction that counts, no need is felt to define concretely the two contrary terms: Europe and China, Europe and Islam, or generally the East and the West. All these "responses" have not been analyzed—far from it. Nonetheless, a fund of shared ideas may already be discerned.

Traditionalist Reformism

The argument here is based on the antiquity of the traditional culture. Europe is a parvenu, one that is still very far from maturity. Its present power is derived from newly acquired borrowings from more ancient cultures (China, India, Islam) whose sciences preceded those of the West. Passing through this early scientific phase, these ancient cultures have transcended it in favor of infinitely richer spiritual experience. The present-day debility of these societies (so the argument runs) is not ascribable to technological backwardness but to deviation from true spiritual goals consequent upon historical catastrophes (usually invasions or conquests: the Manchus in China, the Turks in Arab Islam, etc.). The essential reform is not, therefore, military or political, but moral; the great ancestral qualities must be regained (hence the term "fundamentalist" that is sometimes applied to this current). With a few exceptions, however, European technology is not rejected. Provided that it is stripped of all cultural implications, the adoption of this technology is adjudged necessary. A purely instrumental conception of science is developed; seeking to define its role, the Chinese had recourse to the old antinomy of substance and function; the Arabs had recourse to that of means and ends. It is in the framework of this dichotomy—a return to traditional sources on the moral and political level on the one hand, and technological innovation on the other—that we must situate the Japanese experience, which has apparently reconciled the two contradictory necessities.

II. Birth of the Intellectual

A result of this concession to technology was a deepening of the European influence. Although modern institutions were sometimes closed (Turkey, 1871), in general modern education continued to spread. Students were even sent to Europe (their notes or personal diaries have not yet been systematically studied). What they acquired of European culture was largely derived from books; thus was born the special type of non-European intellectual whose role was to transmit this culture. This book-learned intelligentsia has often been described, both in literature (Dostoyevsky, Conrad, Malraux, etc.) and in political science (where it carries the name of the "new elite"). Actually it seems necessary to distinguish two types: those who had direct access to European culture and those who, failing to master a European language, had to rely on translations. During the historical phase we are considering here, it is this last type of intellectual, still very familiar with his traditional culture, who, if not the most consistent, was still the most effective socially. This period, known as the period of liberalism, saw a timid cooperation followed by an increasing divergence between the two types of modernizing intellectuals. The two men Liang Ch'i-ch'ao and Hu Shih may serve as examples. The first tried to relate isolated elements of European culture to the traditional system; the second judged aspects of the traditional system by setting them against European ideology. The second appears more logical because his system of reference is more effective; the first enjoys a greater influence because he is preparing the way for acceptance of certain Western values deemed indispensable.

The Passage to Liberalism

It is a sign of this transition when the non-European student persuades himself that the goal of European culture is not solely material enrichment. He no longer retains the spirit /matter antinomy essential to the fundamentalist; he acknowledges the value of the European willingness to permit general participation in public affairs. The superiority of the Western politico-administrative machine being no longer questioned, the problem became one of finding the best means of making it acceptable; hence a series of proposals designed to introduce a limited democratization. The very idea of reform had to be made acceptable to a society that had hitherto prized continuity.] The Chinese reformist claimed that the history of China had been one of constant renewals that were occasioned by dynastic changes and disguised as returns to tradition; the Muslim reformist appealed to the Qurʾān, which denies polytheists the right to avail themselves of loyalty to the religion of their fathers. Both the Chinese and the Muslim reinterpreted tradition. Liang Chʾi-chʾao gave a political and economic meaning to the classical doctrine of the Three Stages—Chaos, Peace, and the great Harmony—the last of which was interpreted as the age wherein democracy, prosperity, science, and universal peace shall reign. ʿAli ʿAbd ar-Rāziq turned the notions of *shūra* and *ijmāʿ* into synonyms for democracy. The aim, in both cases, was not so much to prove that democracy had really existed as to make it possible for the future. It was not sufficient, however, to prove that reform is necessary and possible; it was also necessary to show that Europe, too, had had to break away, at a certain moment, from its own tradition—whence the importance attached to the Reformation considered as a rupture and sometimes as an imitation of Islam. These proposals were to justify all constitutional movements in Eastern countries.

The Tragedy of the Liberal Intellectual

To contemporary critics, this argumentation seemed far from cogent; so it seemed also to the intellectual of the second type referred to above. Consistently and rationally liberal, he saw no need to seek this sort of justification. On the contrary, he passed severe judgment on his society's past. He ascribed the failure of this society to "Oriental despotism." In answer to the widely held view that European civilization was materialistic, he replied that a civilization that replaces human labor by the machine is more spiritual than a civilization that fears the machine's competition. Over and above a political liberalism and an unswerving faith in the benefits of education, this tendency was characterized by a pragmatism deliberately hostile to the subtleties of the ancient classical culture; hence the campaign for a simplification of the style, the grammar, and even the script of traditional writing (as in Turkey). The goal of this reform was not only to democratize the culture but also to consolidate national feeling; for the cultural nationalism of the preceding phase had given way to a politico-racial nationalism close to that of nineteenth-century Europe. Thus the universality of Chinese (or Arab) culture had to be done away with in order that the Chinese (or Egyptian) nation might develop. In 1912, Lutfī al-Sayyid insisted on a policy of strict neutrality toward the Turko-Italian war in the clearly envisaged interest of the Egyptian nation. Ziya Gökalp talked of creating a Turko-Muslim culture that would assimilate the mentality and the science of modern civilization.

Concerning this tendency, we may speak of a "temptation of the West": it was a simple reflection of liberal Europe at a moment when the latter was already being attacked on all sides. The careers of these liberals follow similar patterns. After a short experience of active politics, they devote themselves, in increasingly isolated circumstances, to educational tasks. In the contest between Europe and the extra-European world, these protagonists of liberalism, betrayed by circumstances, constituted the only group of intellectuals to live in a situation bordering on the tragic. We need not go far in seeking the cause of their defeat: it was the fundamental inadequacy of the liberal system for a society that did not engender it. That is why some liberals, in despair, returned to tradition—an evolution, already foreshadowed in China by Liang Ch'i-ch'ao, that became more systematic with such a figure as Chang Tung-sun. In Egypt the same evolution is evinced by a Tawfīq al-Ḥakīm. Those who maintain their liberal convictions adopt an individualistic scale of values, increasingly identifying these values with objective reality. Their attitude was actually one of indifference. As we find in Joseph R. Levenson's excellent analysis: "When the traditionalist can be accused of speaking cant, the clear-eyed, unsentimental critic is asserting primarily not the failure of China but the integrity of his own mind, not the dependence of China but the independence of himself. . . . One Chinese gains self-respect by believing a questionable doctrine; but the Chinese who denies this doctrine is not thereby consigned to humiliation. For intellectual honesty is itself an avenue to self-respect."[1] These uncompromising liberals were able to escape, maybe, but they found only increasing isolation (this is the principal theme of Nagīb Maḥfūz's Trilogy).

III. Conversion to Revolution

The social basis of this conversion stemmed from the failure to liberalize the political system and, still more important, from the failure to promote an adequate rate of industrial growth. An embryonic modern bourgeoisie took shape and developed; the other classes, above all the urban petite bourgeoisie, whose number was constantly swelling, fell into a disillusionment as great as had been their earlier optimism. This situation was aggravated by an even more significant development: the spread of unemployment among intellectuals. When this disquieting phenomenon first made its appearance, a genuine "response" to Europe was nonexistent; European culture had become so closely integrated with academic, political, and even social life that the "response" merely reflected an internal dialectic between systems of values motivated by and animating rivalries between social groups. Acceptance or rejection of either of the two cultures, traditional or European, became no more than partial; anticolonial Occidentalism and antitraditional traditionalism gained currency.

The Necessity for Marxism

This transition—whether it is a fait accompli or a process under way or a mere virtuality—has been analyzed at different levels: socioeconomic,[2] psychological,[3] ideological. The

1. *Liang Ch'i-ch'ao and the Mind of Modern China* (Berkeley, 1967), p. 216.
2. Cf. John Kautsky, *Political Change in Underdeveloped Countries* (New York, 1962).
3. Cf. Adam B. Ulam, *The Unfinished Revolution* (New York, 1960).

ideological aspect has important political implications. For a long time it was thought that adoption of socialism as a political program was the result of well-managed propaganda. It is increasingly seen as the outcome of an internal evolution. The two attitudes, fundamentalist and liberal, were opposed yet nonetheless complementary: liberalism was necessary but did not perforce imply a break with the past; traditionalism was a tempting therapeutics but did not resolve urgent problems. Values and history were also antithetical— they had to be synthesized anew, but not according to the old fundamentalist recipes, for evolving society had other needs. "Now, too, we may find a new meaning in the Communist attempt to fit Chinese history into a Marxist time-scale, which is supposed to be also the time-scale of the rest of the world. It is the exact counterpart of the Confucian syncretic effort, as represented in Liang Ch'i-ch'ao's works, to use a Confucian time-scale for world history, to protect China from an inner sense of failure by interpreting its history as part of a universal pattern," concludes J. R. Levenson.[4] Marxism furnished an ideology capable of denying tradition without seeming to surrender to Europe; it allowed one to evade a particular form of European society but did not compel one to return to tradition. Moreover, the individual who adopts it is not called upon, as was the liberal intellectual, to choose between subjective truth and popular belief; he has the possibility of making the two coincide by means of praxis.

A New Nationalism

Where, in confrontation with Europe, the fundamentalist opposed a culture (Chinese, Indian, Islamic) and the liberal opposed a nation (Chinese, Turkish, Egyptian, Iranian), the revolutionary opposes a class—one that is often extended to include all that part of the human race exploited by the European bourgeoisie. One may refer to it as a class nationalism that nevertheless retains many of the motifs of political

4. *Op. cit.*, p. 169.

and cultural nationalisms; hence the difficulties experienced
by analysts who have attempted to define it. Revolutionary
nationalism has three aspects: an exploited class, a dominated
people, and a hard-pressed culture. The opposition to Europe
also assumes a triple aspect.

Western commentators stress the ambivalence of this anti-
European Europeanism; they point to its dramatic character
or allude to psycho-analytic compensation, seeing in it a
possibly useless intellectual acrobatics. Is it altogether cogent,
however, to recall that Marxism was born in Europe? For it
is also true the Marxism offered a critical mirror to a society
bent on imperialist adventurism. The fact is that this society
did not recognize itself therein; it was sometimes to do so on
condition that Marxism be reinterpreted in a certain way. The
attitude of the non-European revolutionary—to adopt on his
own account a truth that was born in Europe but cast aside
by her—is perhaps not so fallacious as it is claimed. In any
case, merely to recall the fact that Marx was a European will
not do.

IV. Redefinition of Europe

Study of the ideological transition from liberalism to Marxism has made possible the defining of a dialectic between
value and history, between particularism and universalism,
between authenticity and alterity. The fact of this dialectic
emerges with increasing clarity as the protagonists themselves
become aware of it. At this point one realizes that, thus
defined, the problem was not a new one as far as the geographical entity of Europe was concerned.

The Russian Problematic

Throughout the nineteenth century Russia had known a
similar debate that had interested and perhaps influenced
Western Europe. It is no accident that recognition of this
similarity came late; it was necessary to wait for acculturation
to develop to the point where China, for example, was
culturally as close to Europe as Russia had been close
geographically. The Slavophile mythology is repeated by all

the cultural nationalists of extra-European countries: the individualism, the pride, the scientistic materialism, and, in the long run, the psychological instability of the Occidentalists—these are the characteristics of all the liberals of the non-European world. The opposing but complementary character of the two tendencies is symbolized by the fact that they continued to divide the intellectual milieu, and sometimes even the individual, almost until the end of Tsarism. The one man who was most profoundly aware of this split, Dostoyevsky, made it the driving force of his great ideological novels. In his speech on Pushkin, he thus expresses the historical need for an ideal synthesis (a need that Marxism was to satisfy): "For what is the power of the spirit of Russian nationality if not its aspiration after the final goal of universality and omni-humanity?"[5] When Marxism began to win over the Russian intelligentsia, it was in process of being reinterpreted by imperialist Europe; in the guise of "legal Marxism," it was at that time little more than a variant of the Occidentalism that revolutionary socialism triumphantly withstood. Would it have triumphed if, in the form of Leninism, it had not been able to satisfy the two needs of particularism and universality: the need to imitate and the need to transcend Europe?

The German Problematic

The generalization does not stop there: the Russians owed this way of conceiving the problem of modernization to the Germans of the Romantic period. It was already the problematic of Fichte and Hegel vis-à-vis the French Revolution, which signified for Germany an enforced reform and an implicit condemnation of German philistinism. Fichte resolved the dilemma by means of an anti-French nationalism with universalist tendencies.[6] This generalization of a dialectic of acculturation, or simply of reform, has not until now been systematized; monographs specifically dealing with

5. *Pages from the Journal of an Author, op. cit.*
6. Cf. *Addresses to the German Nation* (New York, 1968); Hans Kohn, *The Idea of Nationalism*, (New York, 1944).

it are still few and far between, but it is implied in many studies. It has the merit of explaining the adequacy of Marxism to certain situations: Marxism was originally the perfect expression of a similar combination of circumstances, and subsequently it could not but serve as a pattern.

The Notion of Europe

The result is that the term "Europe" can no longer have a geographical, or even a straightforwardly historical, acceptance: the continuity postulated by factual history becomes questionable. The conception that Europeans generally have had of their past—a straight historical continuity from Salamis to the present day—begins to look like ideology pure and simple. The concept of Europe would then denote an economic, social, and cultural formation that has had no less difficulty in conquering geographical Europe than in conquering the rest of the world. This idea is already guiding the investigations of economists and theoreticans of political science.[7] Thus Liang Ch'i-ch'ao and al-Afghānī may have been justified vis-à-vis the naïve consciousness of the Europe of their time.

V. Developments

As yet, direct European influence upon the rest of the world has not overstepped the limits of economics and sociology; history, and above all philosophy, still escape it. Perhaps the game has still to be played.

Revaluations

If it is true that the German dialectic was repeated successively in Russia, in China, in the Middle East, etc., following that "Eastward march" of political revolution foreseen at the beginning of the twentieth century, what is the meaning of this process of universalization consequent upon the enlarging of the world market (the expansion of nine-

7. Cf. G. Almond and B. Powell, *Comparative Politics: A Developmental Approach* (Boston, 1966).

teenth-century civilization?) At what moment does the universalizing dialectic appear on the intellectual horizon of a
given community? What meaning has this appeal of a naïve
and hegemonic Europe to a critical Europe? If these queries
are pertinent, it is the profound signification of historicism,
positivism, and dialectic—systems that are leaning toward
ideology and relativism—that must be reassessed. Over and
above these nineteenth-century acquisitions, we must revalu-
ate the philosophy of the Enlightenment and Cartesianism—
in a word, the very essence of Western culture. This revalua-
tion of itself by the West will have been the result of a
non-European reflection on Europe, but it will be a self-
enrichment, not an about-face of perspective. Can we not,
however, go so far as to envisage the possibility of such an
about-face?

Threatened Rationalism

It must be remembered that the rationale here described
unfolds entirely on the level of ideology: the non-European
finds it in himself through analysis of the culture that he has
absorbed and that is not his own; the European analyst
rediscovers it in the "second degree." Whence the infallible
character of this rationale—an infallibility that is due, perhaps, only to its circularity. It merely reflects an already
established fact: namely, the acceptance of the West as a
master pattern, even if this is an outmoded pattern that bears
little relation to the reality of Europe. It can plausibly be
argued that this pattern will in turn be discarded when it
has served to re-establish a real equilibrium of forces in the
world (for the fundamentalists' attempt to do so before this
equilibrium has been achieved is regarded, even by those
concerned, as a failure).

F. Fanon urges the Third World not to imitate Europe: "Let
us try to create the whole man, whom Europe has been
incapable of bringing to triumphant birth,"[8] but refers imme-

8. Frantz Fanon, *The Damned* (New York, 1963), p. 313.

diately afterward to "the sometimes prodigious theses Europe
has put forward."[9] Which explains, perhaps, why Fanon
seems to have so little influence outside literature. At present
the impulse to call in question the fundamental Western
choice seems largely to originate in Europe itself (psychoanalysis, ethnology, structuralism, not to mention the old
spiritualism). Even Negro cultural values seem to owe much
to the European phenomenon of surrealism (as we see in L. S.
Senghor). One could maintain that any hermeneutic tending
to relativize Western culture is an indirect result of the in-
fringement of extra-European cultures on the consciousness of
Europe. But as yet, apart from circumstantial writings, we
can accredit to no great name of the extra-European world
any radical critique of the fundamental European ideology:
rationalism applied to nature, man, and history.

Yet between Europe and non-Europe there is conflict, open
or concealed. Will this conflict one day give rise to such a
critique? If this should happen, we can at least be sure that
Europeans and non-Europeans together will assist in its
formulation.

9. *Ibid.*, p. 315.

MARXISM AND THE
THIRD WORLD INTELLECTUAL

For the Third World intellectual, who exactly is Marx? Is he the author of some pages on precapitalist societies or the critic of Western society or simply a name under whose authority it is sometimes expedient to place oneself? One could, indeed, cite cases where tactical or academic considerations predominate; such posturings need not be analyzed here. Rather, we shall concern ourselves with the intellectual who, conscious of his singularity, of his culture, of his past, is led willy-nilly to take Marx seriously and to define his position accordingly. Providing the intellectual in question is not an ideologist, in the bad sense of the term, this step is theoretically inevitable.

Who, then, is this Marx of the Third World intellectual? And which Marx? For it will be a specific Marx; he will be read, questioned, interpreted, and understood in a certain way. We must also ask ourselves if the Marx that emerges from this reading is not the re-creation of one stage, at least, in the evolution of the historical Marx. Before replying to this question, I shall briefly explain the meaning of the expression "the Third World" as it is understood in the text that follows. It will not simply designate that part of the world distinguished by famine, illiteracy, and passivity—undeniable characteristics of the Third World today. More exactly, it is to a Second World that we are referring: a world conscious and jealous of its separateness, proud of its traditional culture, a world confronted by a First World (it little matters what we call it) that it can neither wholly reject nor wholly accept. The boundaries of this Second World are subject to change: yesterday it began at the Danube, if not at the Rhine; today it is mainly the area of the eastern and southern Mediterranean; tomorrow it will be central Africa. If it should happen that some part of this world is unaware of its singularity, indifferent to its past; if it has no demands, no pride, no intellectual "misery"; if by chance or by necessity it is accommodating and without bitterness, then we are not concerned with it here. And it will be seen already that this definition implies that problems will be framed on the theoretical level, that they concern the intelligentsia, above all, and that they will pivot on two central ideas: those of history and of culture. It is in this carefully defined framework that the relations between Marx and the Third World intellectual will be described.

I

For a Marxist the most interesting question is everywhere the same: why did he become one? What circumstances did he have to face that gradually oriented him toward Marx? Through the biographies of certain eminent Marxists (unhappily not all of them) we may reconstruct typical formative situations in the Western world and in the Third World. In the former, it is often social considerations that make possible the transition from pre-Marxism to Marxism (whatever the original motives, which are sometimes of a different order); emphasis is always placed on objective, "scientific," practical necessities, which militate in favor of adoption of the Marxist system. In the Third World, on the contrary, the prime motive is never individual happiness, social justice, or economic productivity (though these factors may play an auxiliary role); it is neither purely moral nor merely economic. It is primarily national, cultural, and historical. If Marxism had not logically and necessarily fitted into this perspective or could not have been adapted for the purpose, it would quite simply have been ignored, as were other systems of thought— psychoanalysis, for example—that were and are influential in the West but attract only a few individuals in the Third World, and these unattached to their native milieus. Those who give too much importance to the effects of propaganda are quite simply sidestepping the issue.

The central idea, which will play an important role in the encounter between the Third World intellectual and Marx, is the idea of historical retardation. This is virtually an empirical fact and has no need of elaboration or criticism. In and of itself it already introduces various a prioris: first, that there exists a superior evolutionary stage; second, that there is a unity to history; third, that the only problem to be analyzed is how to compress historical time, which is compressible by definition. Alterity, historical relativism, and the challenging of the notion of history as a directional flow of time—these will come later. Everyday experience militates in favor of historicism,[1] which, defined as the postulation of the direction of history, can be regarded as a primary given for the Third World intellectual. It is not necessary to develop this point at any length here, but it is an essential one, for it is historicism that has determined and probably will continue to determine the relations between Marxism and the Third World intellectual. One may also state that historicism is indissolubly connected to an alerted consciousness and to activism. When these make their appearance in a conquered, dominated, or simply despised and ignored society, it is historicism that is their theoretical foundation. Without it, passivity prevails; stagnation is accepted or granted a positive value. Certain qualifications, however, must be made with regard to the idea of retardation, qualifications that will also

1. The term "historicism" is often given so general acceptance that it becomes difficult to use. In this essay it is used in a limited sense: it refers to the intellectual movement that developed in Germany at the end of the eighteenth and the beginning of the nineteenth century in opposition to the conception of history defended by the philosophy of the Enlightenment. This historicism, historically determined, must be analyzed separately and must not be confused with other movements that subsequently devolved from it in the general context of Romanticism and positive historical research.

apply to the historicism in question. Retardation must be perceived and conceived as recent (not too recent, or it would be imperceptible; not too remote, or the notion would be magnified into one of difference); as secondary (that is, not impinging upon the essentials that define man and life); and, finally, as relating to a single domain. These qualifications change the meaning of the historicist a priori: history is one, but it has different depths. Retardation can be made good because it is not general but relative to a single domain, one that is incapable of diminishing the value of man. A certain superiority is willingly accorded the society in relation to which the retardation exists, because it is postulated that the superiority was bought at a price—the loss, that is, of certain values that the retarded cultures believe they have been able to preserve. The more we study nineteenth-century texts, which have acquired an historical value over and above their circumstantial value, the more we realize how absolutely general this problematic is. It appears in all cultural areas in which the problem of historical retardation has been felt and expressed.[2] Any question of direct influence aside, this agreement merits serious analysis.

At this point we are faced with the issue of the exemplarity of the German experience. The first of its kind, it gives relativity, the acute awareness thereof possessed by the intellectuals—these motifs, spawning every possible response, are gathered in an ideal set of conditions. The exacerbation of the intellectual's anguish, which casts him in the roles of both victim and savior; the constant underestimation of retardation (though it is felt and acknowledged) and a correlative overestimation of the safeguarded values; the obstinate refusal to admit that the world could be divided into arenas of history and non-history, with the contrary affirmation that it is the latter which bears the seeds of universality—this was the recipe for German ideology, whose characteristics of

2. Cf. Hans Kohn, *Panslavism, op. cit., The Idea of Nationalism, op. cit.*; Teng and Fairbank, *China's Response to the West, op. cit.*

idealism, historicism,[3] and dialectic were in every respect diametrically opposed to those of the liberal system derived from the Enlightenment: materialism, rationalist history,[4] and positivism. That the German experience is in fact paradigmatic need not be demonstrated. What has to be explicated is Marx's relation to the problematic of German ideology and to that of its opposite, the liberalism of the Enlightenment.

One could state that Marx abided by this problematic as such; with equal validity one could state that at a certain point he wholly broke with it. But what cannot be denied is that Marx developed in a certain historical context, one that can and must be recreated many times and has in fact been recreated in the Third World countries. Because they think solely in terms of influence, this reliving of Marx is a fact that Western Marxists generally disregard; thus they deprive themselves of any possibility of clarifying the much-debated problem of Marxist orthodoxy. It is impossible to conceive of another, modern Marx who did not know the original Marx. Yet doubtless he alone merits the title of orthodoxy who relives the intellectual conditions that engendered the Marx of

3. Historicism acquires its full meaning only when it is opposed to the rationalist history of the eighteenth century and the liberal history of the nineteenth. The latter, which is a progress-history, gets rid of a large part of mankind's past. Historicism is expressly the reaction to this, for it would save everything because everything has a meaning. Pushed to extremes, as with von Ranke, it presupposes a hidden divine meaning; but Marx separates historicism from mysticism and at the same time redeems progress-history from its superficiality. The many enemies of the "meaning of history" are opposed to the two currents, but even if one considers them both from the Marxist standpoint their critiques seem to affect rationalist history rather than historicism.
4. It is quite to be expected that a liberal like E. Cassirer should credit the eighteenth century with the discovery of the historical world. But it is a far cry from this discovery to that of historical consciousness, which presupposes direct experience of the "objectivity" of history (whatever use is subsequently made of it). In their expectation of imminent changes, the eighteenth-century *philosophes* were too optimistic to feel this objectivity.

history.[5] When such a person discovers Marx—and he will do so sooner or later—he grasps the essential, he perceives the focal point, of the entire system. This explains why Marx comes to the Third World intellectual in and through a context of historicism.

To be sure, Marx did not in fact abide by the problematic of German ideology as such. Moreover, he did not entertain the responses implicit in it. A century has passed, however, and it is evident that he in fact clarified this problematic and raised it to a level where it could be taken up again by others. German ideology did not clearly frame the three paramount questions. These concerned the superior level in relation to which German retardation (the famous German "misery") was to be measured; the possibility of making good such a retardation; and the means of doing so. Nevertheless, it undertook to answer them. The superior level was defined by Jacobinism, regarded as abstract universalization by means of the Terror; the possibility of making good was illustrated by the process of becoming conscious of, and hence accepting, the objective facts; and finally the means could be none other than the intellectual himself. This position postulated that real history is retarded history, in that it alone permits the consciousness that renders history intelligible and sensible. Germany was to follow the path taken by France, and before her by England, but she would do so under the direction not of the myopic lawyers and shopkeepers, but of the philosophers. The problematic was to take many forms: the Romantic embellishment of the Middle Ages, the glorification of the German language, the vindication of the Prussian State, and so on. But the same principles were to animate all these attitudes. Marx of course demonstrated that this way of

5. One often reads that Lenin sought justifications in Marx for actions that in fact had other causes. Would it not be better to suppose that Lenin had already found, noted, and retained those phrases that justified a certain policy he already knew would have to be his own if one day he were to succeed in taking power? We should then be dealing with a total reading of Marx—a reading that ought to be judged as an actualization of Marxist theories.

formulating the problem—or rather of obscuring it—was itself a consequence of that retardation that gives the critic-intellectual the illusion of carrying the weight of history and of being able to resolve contradictions simply by revealing them. In his quest for the real, Marx found, beyond Jacobin-ism, the socioeconomic formation; in the stead of historical retardation, he placed the retardation of the relations of production; in the stead of the intellectual or philosopher, he placed the modern proletariat. One cannot deny that in this framework the fundamental notions of history, revolution, and dialectic apparently remain intact; one may, however, cast doubt on the legitimacy of this translation of the German problematic. Although we are apparently dealing with an identical structure of thought, it is more than probable that the meanings of words change completely in passing from German ideology to Marx's system, and differ-ences in the reading of Marx certainly derive from this misleading resemblance. But the resemblance exists, and it is with this that we are presently concerned, for the Third World intellectual is not likely to dispute it—to him it will seem altogether natural.

For German ideology none of the above ideas presented any difficulties. History was the simultaneous *prise de conscience* of two historical levels that, differences notwithstand-ing, had the same value (the Middle Ages/Modern Times, Germany/France, and so on). Revolution was not transition from one to the other but the safeguarding of the essence of both (the first phase of the French Revolution was not, in this sense, a true revolution, for it had the naïveté to believe in the possibility of a tabula rasa; only the second phase, and above all the Empire, was worthy of the name). Finally, dialectic was the very process by which the transition from one level to the other was effected. History was the act of becoming self-aware *(prise de conscience)*, revolution the realization, dialectic the means. Insofar as they involved a rewriting of positive history at a higher level of consciousness, dialectical contradiction and transcendence were in a certain sense empirical facts whose intelligibility went without saying. After all, dialectic was simply Germany's universalizing of the French experience. But if one considers that all these givens are a prioris of Germany's backward-looking particularism, and if one attempts to find history, revolution, and dialectic at the highest level of historical evolution, that is, at the level of the French and English situations, then they indeed become questionable ideas. Marx's concern to escape from particularism at any price—in this he remained a classical philosopher—cost him conceptual difficulties that it would be rash to assert he altogether overcame.

Marx stops at the socioeconomic formation, where again he finds the contradiction between two levels of reality, the phenomenon of the retardation of the one in relation to the other. History is thus always the history of retardation and of compensation for retardation.[6] By not going beyond the socioeconomic formation, Marx maintains the structure of the German problematic, which is always predicated on the contrasted relations of two groups of facts. A group of facts that is advanced on one level is retardative on the other, and dialectic and revolution are defined by the contradiction and the unification of the two. And it is already apparent that there are two equally valid paths: that taken by Marx, which descends by way of socioeconomic formations, from nation or cultural unity (those famous partial totalities), as conceived by the German ideologists, to class; and that generally taken by the Third World intellectuals, which is the reverse.[7]

6. On this important point see M. Godelier's discussion in *Rationalité et irrationalité*, vol. II (Paris, 1969), pp. 87-94; and N. Poulantzas, *Pouvoir politique et classes sociales* (Paris, 1968), pp. 132-138.
7. The problems posed by the relation between Marxism and nationalism are not therefore only historiographical. "Austro-Marxism" and Slavic nationalism, Lenin and the republics of the Ukraine and Turkistan, Marxism in Cuba, and in Indonesia until 1965, etc.— these pose theoretical problems that seem to derive from the role played by the concept of partial totality in Marx's system. According as one identifies it with a class or a culture, one ends up with two different visions of Marx, one liberal and the other historicist. The problem is to determine how it is possible to make the transition from one to the other, sometimes even without fully realizing it.

But one may also continue Marx's drift and maintain that these motifs are precisely the result of Germany's retardation. One accordingly attempts to situate the fundamental contradictions at the level of the forces of production, other contradictions being no more than aspects or consequences. For a long time this trend was inhibited by fear of mechanicalism, but it seems as if the present situation should be favorable to it. In an economy increasingly dominated by production, it indeed appears that the root contradictions, escaping from the sphere of distribution and of the relations between social groups, have ended up in the sphere of production itself.[8] In these circumstances, the desire to dissociate Marx from his historical background is quite as natural as the desire to redefine his fundamental notions—essentially those of history, revolution, and dialectic.[9] But however interesting these approaches and whatever their future development, the Marx who is completely severed from his prehistory is no truer than the Marx who is seemingly immersed in German ideology and who comes naturally to the Third World intellectual.

It would be futile to seek textual proof that one of these readings of Marx is more valid than the other. The main point is that the difference exists and that it is necessary: the Marx that can play a role in the life of the Third World is the Marx that is faithful to the problematic of German ideology.

It will be asked: Why Marx, and not simply Hegel and Fichte? A preliminary reason is pedagogical: German ideology is virtually unreadable except through Marx. Another and more profound reason is that he saves it from particularism. For the German philosophers, dialectic could be discovered only by a German; and universal history can be none

8. This is J. K. Galbraith's principal thesis (*The New Industrial State* [Boston, 1967]) when he discusses the inverted sequence in which technostructure dominates the market.

9. The importance of L. Althusser's researches stems from the rigor with which he draws all the conclusions proceeding from his initial position (Marx's epistemological break). But would his anti-historicism in principle permit him to reply to the question: What is the historical determination of Althusser's own antihistoricism? And if the question is meaningless from his point of view, how can he enter into a discussion?

other than that of the Germanic spirit (beliefs that the Slavs were subsequently to adopt, replacing Germanic by Slavic, before Marx cured them of these naïvetés).[10] Within the problematic Marx brings a clarification of capital importance: the higher level in relation to which one is retardative is a production system; this, whatever its origin and genesis, cannot be confounded with a nation or race. The problem of compensation does not relate only to consciousness; it is a matter of practical authority. The means of compensation is not a factor outside the production system; it is itself a product of that system. By the same token, absolute denial becomes derisory, for one may be able to confront an army, but not—if one wishes to maintain relations with the outside world—a production system. And absolute submission, which chooses to leave the responsibility to others and takes no part in a world that continues to change against one's wishes, is equivalent to historical death. The *prise de conscience* is still necessary, certainly, but it is no longer sufficient. The Third World problematic, as primary datum for every intellectual living in the Third World, is maintained as a whole and thus necessarily merges into the specific question of action. Clearly, developments of the problematic will proceed in one and the same direction, that of an increasingly pragmatic definition of the means of revolution.

An objection may well be raised: What are you going to do with the evolution that is undeniably present in Marx's thought? For if he indeed began by formulating the issues that concerned him in the framework we have outlined, he was rapidly to become the analyst of capitalist society. National problems at whatever level—economic, cultural, political— no longer constituted independent, still less central, problems for him. Far from seeing the dominated or backward cultures, nations, and races as the prime movers of history, he relegated them to the rank of epiphenomena. The focal point of history was always to be found where capitalism was the

10. Hans Kohn, *The Idea of Nationalism, op. cit.,* Introduction.

most advanced. Furthermore, it is insisted that any return to the original problematic implicit in his preparatory works, a problematic from which he was expressly trying to escape, is a turning back, a simple regression from science to ideology. In different forms this argument has always been adduced against non-European Marxism; it was early the principal argument against Bolshevism, this being regarded as the regrettable victory of provincialism. The objection, which is hard to kill and whose deep-seated rationale is wedded to Western social structure, seems actually to derive from an error of perspective, one that rarely goes unnoticed when any theoretician other than Marx is concerned: that of reading his works solely according to their pedagogic order. It is forgotten that they should in fact be read in precisely the opposite order, reascending from the conclusions to the premises. As it is commonly presented, historical materialism is a result of this error.[11] For analysis of the capitalist system, considered as the most evolved production system, is only a stage; in the following stage one returns to the initial question: How can the backward countries achieve such a system? The relations between economic structure and political action are immediately turned upside down. It is for this reason that Lenin insisted on judging Marx not only on the strength of his theoretical presentation of capitalist society, but also and above all by the political decisions that he never abstained from making (especially in the German scene). The texts used by Lenin to defend his position—texts whose importance he alone saw—show that Marx, even if he did not explicitly

11. J. Plamenatz, *German Marxism and Russian Communism* (New York, 1965), pp. 317-389. The author "regrets" what does not tally with his conservative interpretation of historical materialism. There is no doubt that this historical materialism fundamentally contradicts revolutionary action in the Third World. In it lies what is probably the principal weakness of the orthodox Communist parties: they do not see that at a particular moment Lenin repudiated it. Whenever one speaks of Marxist-Leninism, one is in fact accepting this break, but it is not conceptualized because no care is taken to separate the works of the late Lenin from those of the early Lenin.

return to his initial problematic, having effectively transcended its national context, did not completely abandon it.
Thus, in spite of all assertions to the contrary, it is Marx's
politics as practiced by Marx himself—and not the theoretical
politics that are as a rule extracted from his economic
writings—that allow one to place his economic and historical
studies in their true perspective. For all that, we do not deny
Marx's development from ideology to science. What is denied
is the retrospective reconstruction of an ideal Marx in the
light of the final analyses of *Capital*. The two must be firmly
kept in their historical reality. It is precisely this—thanks to
his situation, which obliges him to recreate the original Marx
who is close to German historicism—that is affirmed by the
Third World intellectual.

However, in completely submerging Marx in the milieu
that produced him, is there not a risk of relativizing him? Will
he not be reduced to a theoretician of historical retardation?
And will not history itself, condemned endlessly to re-create
one and the same historical situation, be impoverished? One
can maintain, and it has been maintained, that the Marx who
is freed from historicism (i.e., who is considered merely the
analyst of the contradictions of the capitalist system) not only
portends the liberation of research in all domains but also
guarantees quotidian history the possibility of enrichment
and renewal. Once again this is the objection raised by
"science," by economists, by social historians, and even by
some philosophers (above all in the West) against the repre-
sentatives of "ideology"—the majority of Third World intellectuals. Despite the confusion resulting from the multiplicity
of adjectives used in defining both groups, one cannot escape
the impression that the fundamental difference derives from
the opposition between two worlds: that of the advanced
capitalist societies and that of the unindustrialized societies.
If to this historicist Marx, to whom the Third World intellectual always returns, there is opposed another Marx, a Marx
of many faces who yet always answers to the developed
world, what then are the relations between the two, what

meaning has their difference, and what impact will this difference ultimately have on the role of Marxism in the world?

These questions become clearer when one considers them at the level of social dynamics; that is, when historicism, born of a certain situation, begins to transform them.

II

In the thoughts of the intellectual living in a backward society the problems of everyday social life take the form of oppositions between two cultures. And because each culture expresses itself at different levels, it is the opposition between different aspects of each of them that is the cardinal fact of daily experience. A host of essays, impressions, testimonies see the light of day, whose authors are preoccupied with weighing and comparing cultural details. These productions are always brilliant, always just, and never convincing. When this way of apprehending the real expresses itself in action, when it is a matter of "reforming" a backward society, the intrinsic fault of this method is confirmed by the virtually inevitable failure of all partial solutions. For a long while the problem of how to modernize, "civilize," or develop will remain. So there is time enough for the culture that is to be assimilated and borrowed to appear successively in all its guises: individualist, secular, humanist, democratic, rational, scientific, materialist, technical, industrial, capitalist, etc.; until finally it is seen as the concomitant, born and developing in well-defined conditions, of a social class—the bourgeoisie. The Third World intellectual, who is the first and for some time the only member of his society to put such questions to himself, is by no means condemned to find Marx along the path he has taken; but he finds Marxian ideas— simplified, abridged, or disguised—in all the books of history, sociology or politics that will generally interest him. With a little luck and critical awareness, a certain threshold having been reached, he realizes that a good part of the modern

social sciences is a simple vulgarization or illustration of
Marx's fundamental ideas.[12] Furthermore, it is modern sociology that impels him toward Marx because it obstinately
refuses to formulate the only problem that seems to him
essential. The definitions, descriptions, and analyses of bourgeois culture, the problems connected with its degree of
systematization, with its origins in the past, etc., are secondary in comparison with the prime question of its transmissibility; anything beyond this concern is already verging on
exoticism. Where the sociology of culture avoids taking a
position, Marx right away distinguishes culture and its social
support; more profoundly, he separates bourgeois culture,
considered as a universal and universalizing value, from the
subculture of the bourgeois class. The latter is a survival from
the medieval past and is as intrinsic to the bourgeoisie as
are the other subcultures to the other classes. Not only does
he make this distinction, but he also clearly draws the
historically necessary corollary: others must assume the
universal bourgeois culture in order that they may save it
from the subculture. For the moment, it is this separability
that is important, not the exact determination of the class
or the group that undertakes to achieve it. For the fundamental question facing the Third World intellectual is precisely this: how is one to adopt the universal bourgeois
culture (embourgeoiser)[13] without first having recourse to the
bourgeoisie? Marx's system at least makes this question
possible.

Opposite Marx we find all the nuances, all the successive

12. See, for example, G. Almond and B. Powell, Comparative
Politics: A Developmental Approach, op. cit., pp. 50-72, 314-332.
Several of the ideas these authors use are extremely obscure if one
fails to trace them back to their Marxist origin.
13. I use the term "embourgeoiser" to designate the act of adopting
and of causing a society to adopt the fundamental elements of
universal bourgeois culture. Other terms, such as "educate," "develop," "Westernize," "Europeanize," are less suitable because of the
extracultural connotations they bear and, above all, because they are
occasionally used to justify the adoption of those aspects of Western
bourgeois subculture that many in the Third World actually reject.

incarnations of liberalism: the Enlightenment, which was the first and the truest; and neo-liberalism, which, defining itself in relation to Marx, has become conscious of its own assumptions. All these currents generally answer our question with the affirmation that there is no bourgeois culture without a bourgeoisie;[14] the universalization of bourgeois culture is possible only through the generalization of the bourgeois type.[15] As this statement is belied by life, there ensues a sort of moral particularism. The neo-liberal henceforth wishes to save himself by himself; the world no longer interests him. This, indeed, is the meaning of the Social-Democratic revisionism that is a liberalization of Marxism, a conservative interpretation of Marx. This interpretation is possible in the exact measure that the type of historical materialism entertained by the liberal is in fact a simple stage in the development of Marx's thought—that in which he systematizes the methodological assumptions of the Enlightenment. It is this that has led some people to find Marx in Montesquieu and to speak of both in the same terms.[16] The bourgeoisie and the proletariat are eternally wedded by liberal and neo-liberal alike, both of whom dissociate Marx from his historical context. The proletariat is certainly the designated successor to bourgeois culture, but in reality its apprenticeship under the tutelage of the bourgeoisie never ends, for the bourgeoisie does not die unless it is guaranteed a new lease of life through

14. Cf. B. Croce, *Essays on Marx and Russia* (New York, 1966), notably the chapter "Of an Equivocal Historical Concept: The Bourgeoisie," in which he constantly confuses universal bourgeois culture, specific bourgeois culture, and the bourgeois class. He finally sees no difference between the two concepts: bourgeoisie and Modern Times. This is, moreover, a polemical position vis-à-vis the traditionalists.

15. There is agreement between the neo-liberalism and anti-Occidentalism of the non-bourgeois countries on the impossibility of transmitting bourgeois culture, and one readily understands a certain attraction between the two movements. Their development, moreover, is simultaneous.

16. The liberal interpretation of Marx is largely accepted and used in studies concerning the Third World. It may be asked if this Marx has not been cast in a role similar to that of "Legal Marxism" in Russia.

the proletariat. The transmissibility of bourgeois culture from one society to another is therefore bereft of meaning, for the entire world must be divided into realms of the cultured and the uncultured, the bourgeoisie and the proletariat. It is obvious that this interpretation demands either a unified history or that societies succeed each other along the same road and obey the same rhythm. And as this conception is belied by events, one falls back on egotism and regardless pride. For the interpretation ever to be acceptable, one has to forget that Marx was primarily concerned with how to replace "German" ideology by "bourgeois" science. One has to forget also that Marx lived long enough to see that Germany, owing to the fact that the bourgeoisie had neither the courage nor the will to be really bourgeois, had become bourgeois under the direction of another class. Unlike other socialists, he did not accept this way out. Although the liberal interpretation of historical materialism may seem plausible (the interpretation actually devolves from Western exclusivism), it is not that of Marx himself. Germany ceased to be a paradigm after 1848, when all sectors of society, under the banner of industry and applied science, simultaneously adopted the bourgeois culture. A half-century of evolution was to show that the center of contradictions had quite simply shifted. If the German Marxists could still believe in the possibility of an *embourgeoisement* by the bourgeoisie (here they were closing their eyes to many disagreeable events), the Russian revolutionaries, still less the Asian, could not.

Studies concerning the history of the Western bourgeoisie would certainly reveal an increasingly comprehensive integration of all aspects of bourgeois culture and an increasingly close correlation between bourgeois culture and class; but analysis of the present situation would primarily reveal a breakdown of this culture. If the historical *embourgeoisement* meant a rationalization of social life embracing all levels of relationships, and if industrial organization, individual morality, democracy, and secularity increasingly appeared as aspects of one and the same world view, then today we are witnessing the emergence of bourgeoisies that are less and less culturally bourgeois, for whom economic rationality is becoming dissociated from private morality, for whom democracy is no longer identical with secularity nor science identical with faith. The more backward a country is, the more will its bourgeoisie fall back on an increasingly particularistic subculture. Dichotomy and compartmentalization will be the distinctive traits. The bourgeois will subscribe to rationalism in the factory, but will be the slave of prejudices and myths in his family and civil life; and when the age of specialization comes, he will have lost even the capacity to feel himself confined in the irrational world surrounding him. The production ethos will give way to the consumption ethos, and in certain Mediterranean countries this new bourgeoisie will quite simply continue to play the role of the old intermediary bourgeoisie of the Middle Ages. This regression will be the more pronounced as time passes. Whereupon the liberal program will no longer find social support, and in terms of method liberalism will be progressively less adequate. Worse, particularism will render it incapable of seeing the problem clearly.[17] Wedded to its axiom—no *embourgeoisement* without a bourgeoisie—it justifies colonization insofar as imperialism signifies only the lending of a bourgeois class to a society that has not produced one. Thus Social Democracy, which represents the liberal interpretation of Marx, has no objection to "civilizing" the world by colonization; it is wholly unaware of the identical process of dissociation between bourgeois culture and subculture that has occurred in the West. It does not realize that the Western bourgeoisie will be incapable of rationalizing the world it has colonized, that on the contrary it will be further exposed to the influence of the irrational.[18] Used at once by and against the bourgeoisie, the irrational

17. If, in spite of everything, the problem is perceived, liberalism collapses—as can be seen in the writings of C. Wright Mills *(The New Men of Power* [New York, 1948], and *The Marxists: 1962* [London, 1963]).
18. It is precisely here and in this framework that an objective analysis of nationalism is possible, and especially of the great politico-cultural nationalisms in India and the Arab countries.

becomes a value in opposition to reason, which deprives the world of color. But the liberal has washed his hands of others' destinies.

Recourse to Marx is, then, unavoidable—but not to the Marx of the liberals, even if they lay claim to a deceptive orthodoxy. In his day, Marx placed no confidence in the bourgeoisie's willingness and ability to rationalize Germany's social life. "Philistinism" continued to flourish, even when the German Empire had become the foremost industrial power of Europe and when German culture and German science were prevailing over the rest of the world.[19] He vested all his hopes in the proletariat, heir to German philosophy, thus seemingly cutting every tie with those who believed that the agent of rationalization might be the critic-intellectual. Is one to believe, however, that he failed to see the uniqueness of his daily relations with the German workers? Granted that Marx did not conceive that a revolution whose goal was the rationalization of social life could be achieved by the intellectuals alone, even so we cannot fail to note the important role he accorded them in the awakening of the working class. Only the intellectual can really discriminate what is universal in the bourgeois culture from what is particular, enabling the workers to adopt the former and to criticize and discard the latter. Dissension within the revolution between the intellectual and the proletarian was already posited as possible. Lenin simply stated that the possibility had become a reality in the special conditions of Russia: conditions demanding the formation of a well-organized group separate from society and whose goal was to assimilate bourgeois rationality in all its aspects. Later, in even more backward societies, this group of revolutionaries was no longer to be simply a party, but an armed force. Separation from the ambient society, which is

19. During the period 1870-1914 German culture probably owed its prestige to its irrational elements, which permitted it to be accepted by both the developed countries of the West and the backward countries. Did not Thomas Mann, moreover, see German culture as the expression of the struggle between Italian rationality and Slavic irrationality?

ever less rational, is still more pronounced. To escape from the bourgeois subculture that everywhere devaluates rationality, it is sometimes even necessary to leave the towns, though these have always been bastions of reason.[20] The more the domain of the universal is narrowed (i.e., made incapable of being generalized through simple osmosis), the more it will be the prerogative of an increasingly isolated group. This group's primary objective will be to reconstruct the center of rationality within itself, a locus that will subsequently spread to include the entire society to be revolutionized.[21]

But then we find ourselves before a new *contrat social*, a new politics of enlightenment, a new Jacobinism against which the German prototypal ideology and historicism specifically arose. Henceforward all roles are in fact reversed and every confusion stems from this reversal. Here we can go no further; for here the Third World intellectual finds himself before mere potentialities. Doubtless he must take a position vis-à-vis these potentialities; but it is not necessary to enter into the details of a hitherto unrealized situation.

III

The historicist reading of Marx, if it is always relevant, is yet not in itself immutable. Once the revolution gets under way, it changes direction and character: it becomes "dogmatic."

20. This is the basic point, common to all Third World revolutionaries (it is sketched by Frantz Fanon and theorized by R. Debray), that liberal or dogmatic Marxists are unwilling to take seriously.

21. The more backward a society is, the more the revolution to be accomplished deepens and spreads. For Arab society, this deepening takes the form of a continuous "traditionalization" that sustains the *salafiyya*, weakens liberal culture, and exacerbates cultural retardation at every level. The result is an impoverishment of Marxism, which continues to play the game, waiting for automatic structural changes consequent upon the civilizing impact of the world market. So the position of the critic-intellectual becomes more difficult, more utopian. All this, understood in practice, still awaits theoretical formulation.

This Marx has often been described from outside—from the liberal point of view, moreover[22]—and is often wrongly considered the product of transitory circumstances or of an individual. The circumstances are indeed transitory, but not accidental. For, appearing in different societies, they are as real as those prevalent in the West and deserve quite as much to be studied. The chief point to remember is that once the revolution begins to be consolidated—that is, once the process of *embourgeoisement* begins under the direction of a restricted group whose prerogative is rationality—the issue of historical retardation is no longer relevant, and consequently the underlying historicism disappears. It is replaced by the vision of history as progress: the vision of the Enlightenment. This means that, in such measure as history again becomes a continuous and superficial temporal flow, dialectic in terms of lived experience disappears. Nevertheless, even with the disappearance of dialectic and historicism, this dogmatic Marxism does not simply come to terms with liberal Marxism, though it recovers many of its aspects—positivism, materialism, history as progress—but all this under the aegis of the past, of the already lived. It in fact rediscovers the ideal type of universal bourgeois culture. But if this ideal type is to be embodied, it must be imposed from above. Time is therefore necessary, and the whole process takes on the dogmatic character of an experimental verification of what is already known: a discovery in reverse. At the same time this dogma is a regulating and directing principle; the entire society is reconstructed in its light. Such a process of confirmation may entail scientific rediscoveries—at best, parallel discoveries (simplifying, more economical)—but never real discoveries.

The result is a new polarization. A neo-liberalism and a neo-humanism, which adopt on their own account the abandoned historicism and dialectic, are reconstituted opposite

22. The best description remains that of H. Marcuse, but it is exterior to its object and actually denies it all objective meaning.

dogmatic Marxism.[23] Meanwhile dogmatic Marxism recovers the positivism of the Marx who anatomized the capitalist system. These tendencies naturally reanimate other tendencies, current in the West, to which they are related; the resulting mixture, variously blended, mostly serves to exacerbate the overall confusion. With its theory of bureaucracy, Trotskyism reconstitutes the allegedly indissoluble couple proletariat/bourgeoisie and similarly reactivates the liberal interpretation of Marx. Dialectical humanism (Lukács and K. Korsh), returning to the historicist critique of revolutionary abstraction, restores historical centrality to the West. The epistemological attempt to define the methodological a prioris of the Marxian analysis of capitalism—an attempt made necessary by the practical difficulties of economic policy—resuscitates the desire to formalize Marx's theories.[24] With the rediscovery of the historical positivity that Western Marxism had encountered much earlier, it would seem that there exists no further difference between Western Marxism and dogmatic Marxism and that a single, undivided Marx might henceforth preside over their reunion. A great difference nevertheless subsists: while both speak in the name of a certain rationality, the Marxist State, imposing rationality from above, is forced to intervene in order to protect it from the floods of irrationality threatening to submerge it at all levels (e.g., family, morality, attitudes toward work); whereas Western Marxism has already interiorized rationalism, which reigns uncontested over the domain reserved for it. When the irrational exceeds its permitted limits, society reacts, even in the absence of State intervention. The first is an ideological Marxism; the second, corresponding to a certain actuality, is more open. More than the differences,

23. The rich content of Trotskyist writings notwithstanding, it indeed seems that their essential point is an a posteriori justification of liberalism.
24. An interesting example is G. Petrovic's *Marxism in the Mid-twentieth Century* (New York, 1967). This critique of Stalinism issues in humanism and epistemology, but only as programs.

however, it is the dynamics of these modes that merit our attention. It seems undeniable that, as revolution develops, dogmatic Marxism draws closer to "scientific" or positivist Marxism: this process is called liberalization, de-dogmatization, humanization, de-bureaucratization, etc. In this sense dogmatism, which is the codification of a provisionary Marxism, is a stage between ideology and "science." On the other hand, the "open," or "scientific," Western Marxism, that of the unfinished *Capital,* probably maintains itself thanks to the existence of this same dogmatic Marxism; for who can positively state that it would not have succumbed, through exposure to multifarious data, to the generalized eclecticism that at all times sustains the activity of the various Western subcultures? The more or less rapid, more or less inevitable, evolution in question does not in the first place interest the Third World intellectual, but he will have to face its reality. He is forced to take it into account when he seeks to define his own relation to Marx.

IV

Thus we may place in its true context the question posed at the end of the first section of this chapter: What is the relation between the historicist Marx re-created by the Third World intellectual and the liberal, or "scientific," Marx as he appears chiefly in the developed world? It seems, indeed, that there is a logical evolution from one to the other that is identical with the evolution traced by Marx himself, but it is also encountered in the evolution of societies. Marxism according to Lenin is originally, and in a certain way, a rediscovery of Marx the German ideologist. The consolidated revolution signals the victory of Engels, of the provisional codification; but this dogmatic system itself dissolves, rediscovering on new bases the liberal and scientific-methodological trends that the West has never ceased to harbor. The Third World intellectual cannot act as if these evolutions had never taken place; he can no longer read Marx "naïvely." If he detaches himself from his circumstances and becomes a cosmopolitan Marxist, he can doubtless equip himself with a version of Marx pleasing to his taste and enter the polemical fray; but his gratuitous eclecticism, as openly flexible and as chatoyant as are many such eclecticisms, will express nothing but his subjectivity. However, if he remains attached to his situation —and it is consciousness of political responsibility alone that can command such a loyalty—he will find himself with no alternative but to re-create the historicist Marx who is indissolubly bound to German ideology. Rethinking history backwards, he will be quick to gain familiarity with the dialectics of relived time, the category of the future perfect. At the same time, however, he cannot fail to realize that he is the third or the fourth to make this reversed itinerary of known orientation and destination. Even to himself his polemic may seem determined by practical considerations. He is defending a Marx of whom he has need, one that is just as unilateral as any other, if not more so. This is what is happening in today's world.

We may now ask: What is common to the liberal Marx of the economists and social historians, the methodological or scientific Marx of Althusser, the ideological and dogmatic Marx of the Chinese publications, the humanist Marx who was Gramsci's and whom many Western philosophers are today rediscovering in their own way (not to mention the Marx of the erudites, the essayists, and the eclectics)? If you choose to disregard the historicization of Marx, i.e., the actualization of Marxist theories that has already taken place in history, and if you are inclined to see a complete absence of logic in the succession of different Marxisms, then you will inevitably remain at the level of interpretative differences, and one may fairly speak of the dissolution of Marx's system. There will be Marx and Marxism just as there is Descartes and Cartesianism, with an infinite gamut of possible re-interpretations.

From the viewpoint of the Third World, one may, however, discern a logic in this succession: one may see each system as the provisional victory of particularism. Every reading of Marx, as is frequently pointed out, must infallibly go from ideology to science. But one may well ask: what science? Up till now it has always been a matter either of a science of the past (the history of social evolutions)[25] or of an analysis of the prerequisites for a science yet to be created (Marxist epistemology); we have not seen the birth of a science of discovery. In the meantime, the only "science" about which the whole world agrees—natural science—continues to prepare a nightmarish future for us at every level of our lives. If this "science," applied to society and defended by Western liberal Marxists, were indeed enriching our lives and increasing our chances of survival and preparing the way for a real universalization, then one could agree that the scientistic Marx ought right away to replace the ideologizing Marx and be adopted by everyone. But none of these conditions has yet been fulfilled.

One must therefore resign oneself to witnessing the role played by ideological, ethical, and humanist Marxism as it emerges from the historicism of the Third World. A theoretical formulation, subsequently abandoned, was made by G. Lukács, who maintained that the sole universal culture was the work of the Western bourgeoisie,[26] in comparison to which all other cultures, whether of social groups or national collectivities, were subcultures. Because the bourgeoisie failed to systematize and never completely assimilated it, Lukács also maintained that universal culture, henceforth separated from the class that was its historical support, devolves upon others, who assume it in order to save it. With the example

25. Many of the results offered by certain historians as verification of Marx's theories seem little more than illustrations, and they are easily faulted by enemies of the "meaning of history," who find little difficulty in demonstrating their circularity.

26. Lukács nowhere gives an exact historical qualification of the universal bourgeois culture that serves him as frame of reference in his critical studies. For this reason these quite often come to resemble "essays."

of Germany always in mind, he describes how this dissociation developed through the reduction of rationality to "science," which in itself serves as an ideology of consensus, an
equalizer of all classes in the cult of a universal abstract. Each
class, however, preserves its particular culture. The result
was not only relativism and particularism, but also (as
experience continues to prove) egotism, philistinism, and
war. Lukács continued his study of the sociology of culture,
but soon ceased to proclaim his pessimistic—it has been called
catastrophic—point of view. This was not only on account of
external circumstances but also because the Lukácsian moment is but a particular moment, interposed between liberal
Social Democracy and dogmatism, of the revolutionary
process. The author recognized that the moment had in fact
been transcended, for he had made the theory of Leninism
before the Bolshevik Revolution, and it was acceptable
neither in the East nor in the West. But the moment could
return, and did so more than once, though it did not again
receive theoretical expression. It is in the light of such a
moment that we may better present and evaluate the historicist Marxism of the Third World. This last may seem a
provincial vision of Marx, but it is basically a reaction to the
imperialist negation cloaked by any dissolution of Marx's
system in the name of science.

There is one reading of Marx with which it is henceforth
almost impossible for the Third World intellectual to reconcile himself: this is evolutionary Marx, whether in the guise
of liberalism in the domain of social evolution or in the guise
of "science" in the theoretical domain. This is the middle-of-
the-road Marx, before he rediscovers his primary question.
At the heart of this reading is the question-begging assertion
that the renewal of history is to be found where the author
of the unfinished *Capital* was looking for it; everything that
happens elsewhere is merely part of the process of making
up for backwardness, i.e., lost time that will count for
nothing in humanity's final balance sheet. The Third World

will always react to this version of Marx as did Europe to the Napoleonic universalization by force of arms; an abstract universalization by imperialism, it masks murderous intentions.

But there is another reading: this is Marx the dialectician, for whom history is precisely that of backward humanity— not, indeed, when it stands in blind denial, but when it consents to follow where progress leads. No one can predict the final outcome of this acceptance; in it alone, however, is hope for a true universalization.

To each his Marx, then? Not exactly, for ideological Marxism tends toward scientific Marxism. This trajectory is always being prepared somewhere in the world, and it is this renaissance and reliving that keeps Marxism always relevant. If "scientific" Marxism could impose itself on the modern world, it would mean that Marx is already a thinker of the past. Marxist polycentricity is a reality that it is useless to deny. But it is the Third World that represents the true focus; without such a focus, polycentricity would be pure liberal relativism.

The Third World intellectual is careful not to reject the other Marxisms. For his part, he propounds a version born of the circumstances in which he lives. The other Marxisms range themselves around his version, in an order now made intelligible by recent historical evolution. He knows that dogmatic Marxism, liberal Marxism, or "scientific" Marxism will someday concern him. But he also knows this: were he to adopt one or another of these forms, he would ineluctably isolate himself from his situation. At worst, he would assist the triumph of relativism.[27]

27. Methodological relativism accepts and even defends, with suspicious ardor, the multiplicity of future paths and models of civilization; but so far as concerns politics it pays no attention to the problems of the Third World and counts above all on the balance of terror to defend the acquisitions and the way of life of the industrialized world.

CONCLUSION:
The Crisis of the Intellectuals
and the Crisis of Society

In the foregoing pages we have described the Arab intellectual's relationships to the past, to language, to culture—in short, to everything with which a society's tradition is concerned. We have described what these relations have been over the past decades, what their present state is, and what they ought to be if the intellectual wishes to confer weight to his words and consistency to his actions.

This book does not treat culture per se. Rather, it treats the problems of Arab society, with culture as the means of approach. The goal has been to lay bare one of the foremost obstacles impeding the evolution of that society. In view of this goal, a description of the intellectual's connection with politics, in the general sense of the term, is indispensable. However important one thinks the crisis of the Arab intelligentsia, it still would not merit the attention it has been given if it did not symbolize and reveal a crisis of society as a whole.

How and why is the Arab intellectual's negativity in keeping with and subject to transposition into state policies that imperil the very future of the nation? How are all the contradictions of society combined in the crisis of the intelligentsia? How does the intellectual's disarray bear witness to the inefficiency and stagnation of society?

I. THE CULTURAL SITUATION

Arab intellectuals think according to two rationales. Most of them profess the traditionalist rationale (*salafī*); the rest

153

profess an eclecticism. Together, these tendencies succeed in
abolishing the historical dimension. But if the intellectual
erases history from his thought, can he erase it from reality?
Of course not; history as past and present structure informs
the present condition of the Arabs quite as much as it does
that of their adversaries. Ahistorical thinking has but one
consequence: failure to see the real. If we translate this into
political terms, we may say that it has the effect of confirming
dependence on all levels. This goes without saying for
eclecticism, which opens itself to every outside influence.
But traditionalist thought is no less dependent, in spite of its
pretensions. Indeed, how can it oppose modern technology,
modern economic and social systems, and modern intellectual
schools, when it is incapable of understanding them and has
not the slightest possibility of inventing competitive systems?
Dependency, visible or concealed, means not only exploitation, loss of liberty, and damage to the pride and material
interests of a nation, but also and above all the continuance
and exacerbation of historical retardation.

Many historians of colonization have subscribed to the
foregoing conclusion; it has been corroborated by economic
studies on countries attempting to emerge from underdevelopment in a neo-colonial framework. Production figures have
actually increased, investments have been made, but the
human, social, and intellectual phenomenon of underdevelopment has not diminished in the least.

This bitter truth notwithstanding, the great majority of
Arab intellectuals continue to lean toward *salafiyya* and
eclecticism and, what is even stranger, believe they enjoy
complete freedom to appropriate the best among the cultural
products of others: the freedom of a Stoic slave! The only
way to do away with these two modes of thought consists
in strict submission to the discipline of historical thought and
acceptance of all its assumptions. We have already defined
the most important of these. Some of them determine "historism": truth as process, the positivity of the event, the mutual
determination of facts, the responsibility of the agents.

Others delimit historicism: the existence of laws of historical development, the unicity of the meaning of history, the transmissibility of acquired knowledge, the effectivity of the intellectual's and the politician's role. These different points have been analyzed more or less briefly in the preceding pages, and we drew the conclusion that today the Arabs may find the best school of historical thought in Marxism, read in a certain manner. Nevertheless, this conclusion is not easily accepted. Submission to the discipline of history is resented by most Arab intellectuals as a loss of responsibility and freedom, inasmuch as the goal of their activity, over and above their specific aims, would already be known. Perpetually to play the role of pupil is in their eyes another slight, since they are asked to play the uncreative role of making good a retardation.

Without irony let us note that these positions are taken by *salafī*, who believe in Providence and are constantly lapsing into the psychology of heroes of the past, and by eclectics, who are at the mercy of every passing fashion. It is hardly necessary to recall that only historical understanding confers logic and density to action; it alone liberates politics from aimless tactical relativism, permitting the individual to conceive long-term plans and to rid himself of the most tenacious illusions. It is impossible to deny that there is a measure of dependency even in this manner of looking at things, but it is transitory; what is more, it is understood. The other ideologies offer that most spurious of liberties, where the very act of repudiation enmeshes one more deeply in the trammels of dependency.

II. ALIENATION IN SPACE, ALIENATION IN TIME

If things are as clear as we have indicated, to what (over and above his psychology) may we attribute the Arab intellectual's indecision, which he has already protracted over decades?

The intellectual is molded by a culture; the latter is born of a consciousness and a politics. Now there are two types of alienation: the one is visible and openly criticized, the other all the more insidious as it is denied on principle. Westernization indeed signifies an alienation, a way of becoming other, an avenue to self-division (though one's estimation of this transformation may be positive or negative, according to one's ideology). But there exists another form of alienation in modern Arab society, one that is prevalent but veiled: this is the exaggerated medievalization obtained through quasi-magical identification with the great period of classical Arabian culture.[1] The cultural policy of all the Arab states combats the alienation of Westernization by two means: the sanctification of Arabic in its archaic form and the vulgarization of classic texts (the resurrection of the cultural legacy). Now, who can fail to see that the fossilization of language and the promotion of traditional culture as a badge of nationality constitute the most decisive means of keeping medieval thought alive, as well as an effective ruse to obliterate from general consciousness the very experience of historical positivity? The *salafī* imagines that his thoughts are free. He is mistaken: in reality, he is not using language to think within the framework of tradition; rather, it is tradition that lives again through language and is "reflected" in him. He will never acknowledge this fact, for it is contrary to his immediate experience; but what linguist or anthropologist would not confirm it? As for the eclectic, his thinking is molded by the categories of a borrowed culture, sometimes in the original language; he is poorly placed to grasp the issues posed by the use of the formal Arabic language and by the revivification of classical culture, and he consequently leaves this capital domain to the unaided intuitions of the *salafī*.

For all objective observers, the true alienation is this loss of self in the absolutes of language, culture, and the saga of the past. The Arab intellectual blithely plunges into them, hoping thus to prove his perfect freedom and to express his deepest

1. This is illustrated by a play on words: *ightirāb* (alienation, Westernization, exile) and *iʿtirāb* (Arabization).

personality. Here, then, are found the inward chains binding him to a present he yet claims to repudiate. Historical consciousness alone will allow him to free himself of them. Then he will see reality, perhaps for the first time. He will see that the absolutes he worships are alien to him, for they may be interiorized only through intellectual analysis and synthesis, that is, through voluntary effort—never through inward understanding and intuition.

It is, after all, astonishing that the notion of alienation, which aims to liberate man from his illusions and to guide him toward the paths of the real, can be interpreted in such a manner that it appears to justify the direst form of exteriority. Here is another proof that Marxism is necessarily colored by the society in which it works, at least at the beginning of its propagation.

The notion of alienation, as is well known, synthesizes four different motifs. First, that of objectification: this permits objective idealists such as Schelling and Hegel to pass from logic to natural philosophy, and designates the act by which the absolute Spirit incarnates itself in nature. Marx emphasized on several occasions that this is really a secularized religious theory. The second semantic content, that of Hegel and Feuerbach, belongs to the philosophy of history: it derives from the transformation of modern philosophy that has witnessed the gradual replacing of theology by anthropology, the closing of the era of religious and metaphysical systems. So man is driven toward the materialism of positive science or Kierkegaardian nothingness—a new polarization that permitted post-Hegelian philosophy to maintain the idea of alienation, since each of the two tendencies (positivist and nihilist) criticized the false divinities worshiped by the other. Nevertheless, before this mid-nineteenth-century polarization took place, philosophical anthropology had restored the liberty of man. From this standpoint, alienation is seen as an abdication by modern man of his capacity for indefinite creation, a surrender to past generations, a dissolution of living humanity into dead humanity. Marx considered this discovery a capital and irreversible conquest; but it was necessary to lay bare its material bases rather than tirelessly to reformulate it.

The third semantic content, reification, is specifically the scientific clarification of a particular form of alienation in a particular system of production. *Capital* analyzes a mode of alienation within a well-defined social framework; ignominious and degrading, it is yet necessary since it makes possible the apprehension, the study, and the transcending of this form, and perhaps all forms, of alienation. Human labor is reified in commercial or industrial capital, which imposes its law as a divinity transcendent to the whole of society (as the cyclic crises dramatically confirm). More profoundly still, the relations between men—their very feelings—are reified. Every aspect of society, including aesthetic expression, takes on the consistency of inanimate things. This form of alienation, however, is peculiar to capitalist society, in which the commercial mode embraces all the intellectual and material products of man, and in which exchange value comes before use value. As Marx described it, the process of reification is not inherent in all societies, whether or not these are based on commercial economy. Above all, it does not make other, more general and deeper modes of alienation outworn or obsolete. Nor is capitalist reification the essence of alienation; that is, its absence does not necessarily dispose of all alienation; it is merely an historically determined form of it.

The fourth semantic content is ideology or false consciousness. This devolves from the preceding content in that it supposes the division of society into classes and the transcendence of capital, which is seen, analyzed, and studied as a self-creating force. Thus, the scientific enterprise itself having gone astray from the outset, escape from false consciousness is possible, according to Marx, only by the ideological critique of reification. This laying bare of the screening activity of capitalist man can be effected only by going back to the base of capitalism, that is, to the commercial mode, and by employing the sole effective rationale, that which posits man as an historical self-creating being. *Capital's* power of persuasion resides in the fact that it is the historici-zation, the integral dynamization, of bourgeois political economy. Marx took precautions to ensure that none of the mystifications exposed by Feuerbach would surreptitiously enter into his system while he was dismantling the traps of bourgeois consciousness.

We can now see how the Arab intellectual, whether he is *salafī* or eclectic, reverses the terms of the problem. He insists upon a form of alienation that he rarely experiences in the course of his public life, and passes over in silence the forms of alienation into which he is continually plunged.[2] He comments favorably on Marx's analyses, yet turns back in adoration toward a distant past. He reprobates the Western intellectual with his alienating dependency on the capital and ideology of the dominant class, yet he willingly abets his own dissolution in the absolute truths of the medieval world: al-Jāhiz's language, al-Ashᶜarī's scholasticism, al-Ghazālī's mysticism, and so on. If we continue to associate, as we nearly always do, the future of the Arab peoples with fidelity to these absolutes, then we shall have to conclude that Arabizing (or medievalizing) alienation is the worst of all and that the campaign waged for so many years against the alienation of Westernization (a successful campaign, it must be acknowledged) serves only to camouflage an ever-growing cultural retardation. Who can deny that the price of this campaign has always been too high: lost time, accumulated retardation, successive defeats, and ultimately the drift into ahistoricity.

III. THE ROLE OF THE PETITE BOURGEOISIE

Medievalization is the result of a cultural policy, but whose policy? With this question we have reached the social basis

2. Here one sees a specific consequence of negative ideological influence exerted by philosophy regarded as a formal educational training, for this confusion was facilitated by the fact that Sartrian thought has been very influential in Arab university circles. Marxist alienation was always interpreted by way of existentialist givens.

of a cultural situation that, despite its destructive aspects, is self-perpetuating.

We offer here a few brief remarks that make no claim to get to the root of the matter. The vast domain of the Arabs comprises a baffling diversity of circumstances; only specific localized studies (and these not necessarily within the framework of the organized states) will achieve significant results. I shall limit myself to observations drawn from experience of the Maghrib; from these the reader may generalize where he sees fit.

I have described elsewhere the principal characteristics of the national State dominated by the petite bourgeoisie, whose ideology is "technologism" and whose mainstay is a closed bureaucracy closely controlled by its primary means of centralization and defense: the army.[3] Nasser's Egypt and Ben Bella's Algeria have served as prototypes. Since then, many other Arab states have reached this stage—notably Syria and Iraq. Other states, such as Libya, the Sudan, and South Yemen, which might seem to qualify, do not altogether merit inclusion on account of the weakness of their bureaucracies and hence of their States, or on account of their economic and demographic weakness; for foreign policy and explicit ideology are not defining criteria of the national State. On the other hand, one may say that Iraq is beginning to differentiate itself from the type in question; it is, however, too early to forecast the type of political organization it will ultimately adopt should the present coalition of progressive forces succeed. Therefore we may say that the type of national State we have described, some bold but marginal experiments in the Arabian Peninsula notwithstanding, continues to be the most advanced form of political organization in the Arab countries.

Let us be quite clear on this point: the petite bourgeoisie, which politically dominates the national State, takes first place in all Arab political entities, even when it possesses neither power nor economic preponderance nor military

3. See *L'Idéologie . . . , op. cit.,* p. 5 ff.

backing. In countries such as Morocco, Saudi Arabia, Jordan, and the Gulf Emirates we find public administration, the technical services of public and private organizations, teaching, and culture in the hands of the petite bourgeoisie, so that, in power or out of power, it is this class that delimits the intellectuals' horizon and defines cultural policy.

So we find a close connection between the petite bourgeoisie and the cultural situation we have described above. Let us pose, then, a very awkward question: What is the petite bourgeoisie? This question, let it be added, has been central to the enquiries of progressive Arabs for the past twenty years, especially since the failures of Nasserism have multiplied.

In the classical Marxist analysis the petite bourgeoisie does not deserve the name of "class." One may even say that Marxist objectivity (opposed to the utopianism of the other socialisms) is expressly predicated upon the negation of the petite bourgeoisie *qua* class; it is seen as a nondescript residue of decadent classes, or it may be negatively defined as what remains indeterminate in society after one has positively defined the classical trio: landed aristocracy, bourgeoisie, proletariat. To be sure, these are logical categories rather than classes—the latter can be diversified and subdivided within the same economic categories. But, as an historically and sociologically determined group, the petite bourgeoisie may not be assigned to any such category. Though it is true that the petite bourgeoisie is absent from *Capital*, it is abundantly dissected in Marx's historical and political works. In these, it is characterized essentially by an intermediary position: it is neither a proletariat, since it still possesses a means of production, nor a bourgeoisie, since it does not possess enough capital to make regular use of salaried labor. It is chiefly composed of artisans, peasantry dependent on family work forces,[4] shopkeepers, and poor intellectuals. The feature all these groups have in common is economic indepen-

4. A confusion that is rarely clarified in contemporary Arab political thought is that which persuades us to speak always of a peasant class. The consequences can be easily imagined.

dence, this being made possible by possession of the means of production. But if we accept this feature as the distinctive criterion of the petit-bourgeois condition, we are left with a formal criterion that lumps together such disparate realities as a plot of ground, tools, a herd, monetary capital, an education. For this reason Marxists have considered the petite bourgeoisie as a heterogeneous collection of groups and subgroups and have always stressed its penchant towards utopianism, adventurism. Strangers to the productive mode, the petit bourgeois have no means of familiarizing themselves with the rationality of science and industry. Crushed by the capitalist system, which they apprehend from outside as a destiny, they long to react against it from outside, to destroy it by willful violence. Having no future in the dominant system,[5] they return to an embellished past where they see themselves as masters of their own destinies; even as socialists they are oriented toward the past—as we see in the beginnings of European socialism. It is because the proletariat is objectively unified, organized, and severed from the past that Marx links its development to the future of modern socialism. Any tendency towards opportunistic individualism is the result of petit-bourgeois influence and must be ruthlessly combatted.

This is a well-known analysis, which does not, however, give exact answers to our question. Can we, in point of fact, apply them to Arab society? No, for they apply to societies that capitalism has, to a certain point, succeeded in unsettling. If the petite bourgeoisie is not a clearly demarcated class in advanced capitalist societies, then it is still less so in a fragmented and heterogeneous society. It is necessary, then, to describe each petite bourgeoisie in its particular historical and economic context. In Arab society, the three clearly demarcated classes are numerically and socially weak. The petite bourgeoisie, far from being residual, is in the majority

5. At least during the beginnings of capitalist development. Later on, subtle channels of reconversion make the system bearable to the petite bourgeoisie; this is the whole evolution of Social Democracy toward an increasingly acknowledged liberalism.

in certain strategic sectors and has before it an objectively discernible future: in commerce (in consequence of accelerated urbanization) or in farming (in consequence of the extension of private property, whether by colonization and irrigation or by the land distributions of agrarian reform).

In the Arab countries of today, the petite bourgeoisie can be characterized thus:

——It represents the majority of the urban population, so that town life is synonymous with petit-bourgeois life, above all when the economically or politically dominant class is a foreign one.

——It indeed represents a minority in relation to the mass of peasants; but these, insofar as they leave the communal framework to enter a cash economy, transform themselves into small independent landholders before social differentiation reinforces the large and middling properties and increases the number of agricultural workers and landless peasants; they consolidate the power of the urban petite bourgeoisie since both classes share an attachment to independence and to private property.

——Generally speaking, it is the exclusive repository of culture, traditional or modern. True, there is a difference between the traditionalists and the modernists, but all benefit from an identical social position.

These characteristics and others (less visible) pointing in the same direction explain why the petite bourgeoisie must necessarily come to power and why through its exercise of power it perpetuates a general dualism: economic, social, cultural, and linguistic. It comes to power easily because the three classes—aristocracy, bourgeoisie, proletariat—are either foreign or numerically weak and because the peasant majority is separated into two groups: one of these shares the petite bourgeoisie's values and the other is little prepared to participate in political life. As for the dualism, it is really a principle of action; more exactly, it is but the ideological and political expression of the petite bourgeoisie's social situation. On the one hand it profits from modern culture (assimilated in the original language) by economically and militarily consolidating its power; on the other hand it profits from its fidelity to traditional culture by legitimizing an exclusive authority. Let us not forget, however, that the petite bourgeoisie is not a logical and economic category, but an historical category; it is not a class, but an aggregate of groups united by common values—whence an instability that derives from internal struggles but remains within the framework of an identical power structure.[6]

This short analysis does not pretend to explain the convulsive nature of Arab political life, but simply to throw some light on the relations between the social and cultural situations; thus we may hope to find some answers to the question asked at the beginning of this essay: How has traditionalist thought been able to maintain itself so long, and in what context might it be transcended? In a preceding chapter we compared—and sometimes assimilated—historical consciousness, the rationalization of social life, and political efficiency. Now let us pose the question in a different form: How, in the framework of political domination by the petite bourgeoisie, can historical consciousness be propagated and social life be rationalized? The essential fact here, let it be stressed, is dualism, particularly in the cultural domain. And if from the outset we have opposed the traditionalist intellectual and the eclectic intellectual, it is because this contradiction expresses and exhausts a dualism that is at once an observable fact and a policy.

All the agents of modernization in industry, in administration, in the army, in education, come from these strata of the petite bourgeoisie and are influenced by foreign schools of thought; they are often culturally formed by a foreign language. Yet they represent a minority within the petite bourgeoisie, and a minority within a minority within the total

6. In this sense, analysis of the contradictions of the Nasser regime in terms of directly discernible class struggle seems hardly convincing. A whole theory of mediation is requisite, one that would make of the directing group a mirror of all social contradictions. Such a theory has not yet been formulated with sufficient rigor.

population, upon which they have not the slightest influence; they have, moreover, little desire to exert any influence, leading the isolated existence of satisfied consumers.

The group in power pursues an educational policy that consciously aims to deepen this dualism. The scientific, technological, commercial, and other institutes, which prepare students for service in the modern sector, offer (frequently in a foreign language) the most advanced programs and methods. Thus is educated, on a pattern different from that of the nation at large, a bureaucratic elite that is detached from the population and committed to the service of the State. This last is an abstract entity that conceals the power of that sector of the petite bourgeoise from which the elite itself derives.

As for the other educational institutes (humanities, law, theology, etc.), either they remain faithful to the traditional methods or they are dedicated to defending the same values in a slightly updated manner. Traditionalist thought therefore, be it predominantly religious or predominantly cultural, reigns everywhere. From these establishments comes the intellectual elite (teachers, writers, journalists, preachers, etc.), besides the greater part of the political elite (members of the parliaments, of the parties, of numerous committees, etc.). By its very existence this generalized duality guarantees the perpetuity of traditionalist thought; for it knowingly maintains the preponderance of the traditional sector and allows the petite bourgeoisie to preserve the leading role in the domains of politics and culture.

The situation may be summarized thus:

——The Arab petite bourgeoisie is characterized by an assimilative, utopian, and eclectic mentality, as are all petite bourgeoisies.

——Possessing political authority, or at the very least cultural preponderance, it imposes the above characteristics as values upon the totality of society.

——Being a minority, a fraction of which is able to govern by virtue of its monopoly of modern culture, it perpetuates the status quo by the sole fact that it keeps itself in power, giving this culture to a tiny minority that is quickly cut off from the rest of the population. Modern culture is thus a means, a tool, an ideology subordinated to traditional culture, where the latter is propounded as an intangible value.

These points permit us to explain the permanence of traditionalist thinking. Accordingly we may ask: Is it possible to escape from this enchanted circle? Can the Arab intellectual who is forced or who chooses to remain a member of his society nevertheless transcend the limits imposed upon him by politics? If this transcendence is indeed possible, how and by whom may it be effected?

IV. THE CHANCES FOR RATIONALITY

The political elite directing the national State, the traditional or modern intellectual elite, the civil or military bureaucracy, the technocratic stratum, etc.—none of these groups, all of which belong to the petite bourgeoisie, wishes for or seriously imagines a victory of modern over traditionalist thought. No one would like to see modern rationality overstep the limits of the factory, the public bureau, or the office and enter the sociopolitical domain.[7] Each of these groups has special reasons for persevering in its hostile attitude, but the underlying motive should be sought in the general attitude of the petite bourgeoisie as a whole.

These are abstract assertions that will have little explanatory value unless they are substantiated through detailed studies. Yet if we provisionally concede that they quite faithfully describe the prevailing situation in the Arab countries, then we must recognize that the chances for a general rationalization of Arab society are very much reduced and even unlikely, for the system carries within itself the efficient cause of its perpetuation.

7. In *L'idéologie arabe contemporaine* I stressed the rationalizing role of the petite bourgeoisie as compared to the groups that preceded it in power. Here the judgment is the more severe in that we are taking into consideration the exigencies of the world situation.

Hence we urgently require answers to the following questions:

1. Is the army—the striking force of the urban and rural petite bourgeoisie—capable of rationalizing society in a way that is both vigorous and orderly?

2. Is the dominant party, which organizes and directs the activities of the various petit-bourgeois groups, capable of comprehensively rationalizing public life?

3. Can the bureaucratic sector, which lives like a bourgeoisie but retains a petit-bourgeois mentality, rationalize society?

4. Is the working class, which grows and develops in the shadow of the politically dominant petite bourgeoisie, capable of rationalizing itself in order that it may do likewise, through osmosis, for the rest of society?

5. Can the intellectual elite, which fashions the petit-bourgeois State, transcend the narrow confines of its immediate interests and of the ruling elite's immediate interests and bring itself to desire a society that is better prepared for rapid evolution?

At present we can reply to none of these questions with an unqualified "yes." To be sure, it is the fourth question that poses most of the problems, since it is customary for progressives everywhere to base their hopes on the working-class movement. But reality is always unamenable to the simplifications of revolutionary romanticism. We must pay serious attention to the conditions in which the industrial working class of each of the Arab countries is born and develops. We must begin with the postulate that a proletariat born in a national State dominated by a modern national bourgeoisie cannot resemble an emergent proletariat in a dependent society administered by a foreign bourgeoisie or in a State dominated by a local petite bourgeoisie. The following specific questions must be asked about each separate working class: How far is it independent of the petite bourgeoisie, and especially of the artisans? How far is it conscious of its specificity qua class? How far has it an independent direction?

What is its relation to the technocratic stratum? What is the structure of the factory, what language and what training methods are used therein, etc.? It is only after having given the most realistic answers to these and many other questions that we may decide whether or not the proletariat is capable of interiorizing rationality and whether it will afterward succeed in imposing it on the ambient society. So far as the proletariat of the Maghribian countries is concerned, and confining ourselves to outward observation alone, we would be tempted to answer "no" to all the above questions. Numerous, and for the most part organized within powerful syndicates, this proletariat nevertheless needs education in the ways of rationality inasmuch as the factory has yet to be democratized, Arabized, made autonomous, which presupposes, rather than conditions, a political revolution.

What can be said of the intelligentsia, in the strict sense of the word? It is socially defined in the following manner: petite bourgeoisie > bureaucracy constituted by different groups > intellectuals > revolutionary intellectuals. The revolutionary intellectual, necessarily of petit-bourgeois origin, belongs to a small minority of that uncommitted intellectual elite that is satisfied with expressing its lived situation and does not attempt to transcend it even in thought. Now, a role falls to this revolutionary intellectual; historically determined by the practice of others, this role is a possibility—not a transcendent duty or a destiny. It may or may not be filled, just as Arab society may someday be modernized or may drag out the moribund existence of an alleviated Middle Ages. The role consists in presenting the general program of modernization of Arab thought and society.

Preliminary questions immediately come to mind: Is there a real chance that this type of intellectual will appear? Why will he feel it necessary to transcend the present situation? How will he fulfill the above-mentioned role?

It may be thought that the foregoing discussions make the emergence of a positive and historically-minded intellectual seem improbable. Yet if this type does appear, he will owe his existence to the hegemonic situation characterizing the world of today. If the national State were able to sever all foreign relations, it would indeed be impossible for such an intellectual to emerge. It remains true, however, that international competition and external threats force the national State to maintain certain international relations. Although these remain under close surveillance and within specific areas (the army, industry, scientific research), in spite of everything we are in fact witnessing the introduction of certain information, certain ideas, certain approaches. Comparisons with what exists elsewhere in the world *can* lead the Arab intellectual beyond romanticism toward positive thought.

As for the concern that could impel him toward this act of transcendence, we find it in in the national feeling that is the very foundation of the official ideology of the national State: the intellectual becomes a revolutionary when nationalist awareness of the reality of the outside world replaces unconsciousness or self-willed blindness. Here is so natural a possibility that one cannot a priori deny it without sufficient proofs.

How can he play his part? By once and for all repudiating the romanticism, the utopianism, and the exclusivism of the petite bourgeoisie; by taking a clear and distinct position vis-à-vis language, history, and tradition; by becoming aware of history. We have frequently referred to this last point in the foregoing pages, which are intended primarily for those Arab intellectuals whom circumstances have permitted to depart from the magic circle of petit-bourgeois consciousness. Such intellectuals will necessarily be few and clearly will not be able to modernize Arab society by themselves. But let us not forget that the petite bourgeoisie is a minority in the long run. There are other groups—landless peasantry, workers. Even within the petite bourgeoisie there are racial or cultural minorities that have no interest in seeing the present situation perpetuated—especially as it accumulates failures within and without. These groups can objectively transcend the limits of the national State, but they have always lacked the organization, the will, and the intellectual training that would enable them to imagine an order different from the one in which they live. Some of them are probably ready to accept any program that can show them a convincing image of a different order, one more open to the future. Although education is kept under surveillance, although information is censored and culture manipulated, the system is not perfectly closed and cannot be. It falls therefore to the revolutionary intellectuals, however small their number, to hold ready that program that is capable of guiding the Arabs toward the paths of the future.

Let us say plainly that this program does not exist today. Clearly it has nothing to do with the economic program offered by the "local" progressives in each of the Arab countries, nor is it the rhetorical program of those who believe that Arab unity is an accomplished fact rather than an eventuality or a possibility. The former lacks historical depth, the latter lacks rationality. We are referring to a total program that adopts a clear and consistent position toward the absolutes of traditionalist thought, the problems of minorities, democracy at the State level and at the level of local communities, unity in its real historical framework, the national State and its primarily cultural policy, etc.—in short, a program giving a rational analysis of the past, the present, and the foreseeable future of the Arabs. Thus at last will traditionalism and eclecticism be truly defeated and transcended.

V. OUTSIDE OBSTACLES TO RATIONALIZATION

To abandon *salafiyya* and to surpass the limits of justificatory nationalism is a very arduous task for the Arab intellectual. This difficulty is compounded by an outside obstacle, one that creates a true inhibitory complex. Even if he succeeds from time to time in going beyond traditional nationalism, this complex deters him from following the spirit of history and incites him to turn back. This obstacle is related, one suspects, to the Arab problem par excellence, that of Palestine.

Many foreign observers have declared that the Palestinian affair was the factor that shook the Arab world out of its somnolence. In support of this statement, they cite the military coups d'état in Syria and Egypt that followed the unhappy outcome of the 1948 war, the fall of the Iraqi monarchy and the birth of the United Arab Republic after the Suez crisis, and the fall of the Libyan monarch and the wave of nationalizations following the June 1967 war.

These are undeniable facts. Yet they show only one side of the question. The events referred to were all reactions to political or military failures and were to a certain extent improvised (not as tactical moves but inasmuch as they did not form part of an overall strategy). As retaliatory acts without an ideological foundation, they had in the long run only a mediocre effect on political education.

One may go further and maintain that the Palestinian affair has had the effect of reinforcing traditionalism, first ideologically, then politically. The above-mentioned reforms were not conceived and presented in a framework opposed to traditional thought; on the contrary, they often drew their most persuasive justification from it. This was an ideological gain for the most fiercely conservative states.[8]

How exactly did this strengthening of tradition come about? First, by the political utilization of the very existence of the Zionist State as a tangible proof that modern science and religious nationalism can coexist. The traditionalist thinker has even been able to turn the Arabs' defeat to his advantage. To one who maintains, as I have maintained in this book, that modern science is intimately linked to democracy, secularism, historical thinking, etc., the reply is: "Look

---

8. Here we must take a pure "event" into account: the discovery of rich petroleum deposits in the least populated and the least developed areas of the Arab world. It is this unequal division between material and intellectual riches that, in a unitary framework, works against the progressive countries.

around you. Don't you see that the Zionists have constructed a system in which technology, militarism, and religious and cultural nationalism mutually strengthen one another? You, who are always appealing to reality, must concede that this is a reality that militates against you." In fact the *salafī* often confuses appearance and reality, namely, what the Zionists believe themselves to be and what they are; but his argumentation is tremendously effective because it appeals to simple common sense. The bare fact, impossible to deny, is that Israel by its very existence has checked the Arabs' progress and has been one of the determining causes in the process of continual traditionalization. All liberal, secularizing, and progressive thought appeared as a ruse of Zionist and imperialist propaganda. Nothing more clearly demonstrates this cultural retreat than the campaign recently launched against the founders of the moderate *salafiyya* themselves, al-Afghānī and ʿAbduh—this from the most conservative milieus.[9]

Let us note also that the existence of Israel has weakened the Arab liberal and progressive movements and hence has gradually discredited the whole liberal democratic idea. Intellectuals who were enemies of the status quo were thrown back on romantic or anarchist ideologies—a fatal turn in the history of modern Arab thought. Progressive intellectuals form a minority of the Arab intelligentsia; even if, through a favorable combination of circumstances, they succeed in transcending the petit-bourgeois point of view, they make their way with difficulty on account of the counterpressure exerted by the Palestinian problematic. Why?

Here we have no alternative but to acknowledge a real external influence. In a preceding chapter we outlined the reasons for the superiority of the Zionist over the Palestinian plea. It remains nonetheless true that the world does not grant the Arab position an equitable hearing, even when this

9. As strange as it may seem, this campaign gained support from the very critical works of Elie Keddourie, Sylvia Haim, Nikki Keddie. These are summarized by Albert Hourani in his *Arabic Thought in the Liberal Age* (London, 1962), recently translated into Arabic.

position is presented in a purely historicist framework and is
no longer predicated on an immutable and transcendent right.
It is also true that only a minority presents its case in this
manner, and one would be justified in treating it as exceptional; but having said that, we must straightaway add that
the outside world, Eastern and Western, socialist and capitalist, does not use the same logic, does not judge the Arab
position and that of their adversaries according to the same
yardstick.

When the Arab intellectual calls his fellow countrymen to
rationality and to historical awareness, he takes his stand
solely on the fact that he speaks in the name of a potentially
universal logic, but when it comes to treating the problem
that most concerns him, he cannot fail to recognize that the
world is not always faithful to that logic. It complies with
logic when logic militates against Arab interests, and rejects
or ignores logic when it tends to favor them. So it is easy for
the antirationalist intellectual to reply that historicism means
realism and realism means submission to the fait accompli.
And he takes refuge in romanticism and ahistorical voluntarism.

Let us recognize that vis-à-vis the Jewish question neither
East nor West has a position that is reducible to rational
logic. Over and above the partial justification one often hears
(the economic role and vote of American Jews, the strategic
position of Israel, the cultural and scientific role of Jews in the
U.S.S.R., the national feelings of Eastern European Jews, and
so on), it is not difficult to sense deeper, perhaps repressed
reasons. Even these rational justifications are irrational in the
eyes of the Arabs, since the Arabs play no part in their
genesis and have no power to change them. What are they to
do if American Jews have concentrated in the large cities and
have thus won political power disproportionate to their
numbers? How can it be helped if Soviet intellectuals and
scientists include a large number of Jews? (Supposing, of
course, that these facts really influence the policies of the two
superpowers.) That the secular West and the socialist East can
support Zionist ambitions that directly contradict their pro-

fessed ideologies is a fact that weakens the progressive Arab intellectual's position from the outset.[10]

That is a truth that has to be emphasized; having done so, we must yet return to the necessity for rationality; for to seek refuge in romanticism and anarchism, blasphemous poetry, verbal revolutionism, has but one consequence: the strengthening of the traditionalist mentality, which has been and always will be the root of a compound retardation. The progressive Arab intellectual must accept the Palestinian drama as a fact and the attitudes of others (rational or irrational) as facts, and he must define his position with regard to the cardinal problem of the Arabs: their historical retardation. He must not invert the terms by defining his position vis-à-vis historical retardation with an eye to the attitudes of others vis-à-vis the Palestinian question. This is a difficult position, certainly—in the present circumstances even heroic. Without taking it, however, there is little hope that the Arabs will find their place in the modern world.

VI. A FINAL WORD

The Arab world has known but one revolution—the national revolution—that comprised several others: intellectual (the discovery of the worth of human individuality), social (the discovery of democracy), economic (the discovery of social calculation and the concern for production). But because of this very confusion between goals and aspirations, none of them has been truly realized. The Arab society of today is heterogeneous: different epochs, temporalities, and humanities are placed side by side therein. Believers in continuous revolution use this indistinction to justify their desire to compress time. However, this compression necessarily implies that all the attainments of the successive revolutions of modern history should be ideologically interiorized. The idea of continuous revolution means two things: it means that on

10. Note that this development implies a contradiction, on both sides, between value and history.

the level of ideology the various phases of development are inescapable; in practice, it implies the possibility of bypassing certain phases. It consequently supposes the effectivity of the role of the intellectual minorities—otherwise it is meaningless.

The more a society is retarded, the more its revolutionary elite should be cultured, progressive, conscious of all the qualitative leaps that have occurred in the life of humanity. In the modern period humanity has experienced a religious reform, a democratic revolution, an industrial revolution. Each of these has expressed, in a particular domain, the evolution of society as a whole; from them derive breaks in thought (also called revolutions)—scientific, rationalist, historicist—that have given rise to ideologies whose most complete expressions were liberalism and Marxist socialism.

The more a society lags behind other societies, the more are the goals of revolution diversified and deepened; the more the intellectual is conscious of this retardation, the greater are his responsibilities and the more frequent are temptations to escape into illusion and myth; the more a revolution must be all-embracing, the more distant and improbable it seems. Such indeed is the situation of the Arab revolutionary. The various struggles for freedom—individual, communal, national—which the bourgeoisie of the national State nowhere forced to a conclusion, now devolve upon him. If things remain as they are today, the Arabs' retardation, despite an ever-increasing gross national product, will be exacerbated—linguistically, culturally, ideologically. Foreign Marxists will increasingly tend to believe that the Arab revolution is unattainable; and when it finally happens, it will be reckoned fortuitous.

Confronted with this less than encouraging situation, the Arab intellectual must objectively appraise what he has hitherto called his political commitment, which has often induced him to play hide-and-seek with his convictions for the sake of practical results. His only truly positive role is to be radical in the exact sense of the term—whatever the short-term cost. The ideological and cultural front has always been

calm in the Arab countries, because this is a domain in which
all social strata have coexisted in a common adoration of
absolutes. If this calm endures, it is likely that the Arabs will
be the last to wake up to history—perhaps sharing this
destiny with the Indians, who, since Gandhi, have likewise
taken the religion of tradition as a national ideology.

To put an end to the traditionalist mentality requires much
modesty; above all, it requires acceptance of a common fund
of ideas and a willingness to identify oneself only through
one's *tone*. Our modern culture will be derived; let us accept
the fact if it is the path to realization. We must in any case
pay the price of a long decadence. We have already paid
heavy tribute to an empty cultural nationalism that is all the
more distressing when one thinks of the extraordinary modesty—perhaps feigned—of the Chinese, as they at last realize
the dreams of several generations of intellectuals fated never
to see the coming of the day. Strange indeed are certain
proclamations announcing a special competency in the art of
manufacturing "civilization!"[11]

All too long has the Arab intellectual hesitated to make
radical criticisms of culture, language, and tradition. Too
long has he drawn back from criticizing the aims of local
national policy, the result of which is a stifling of democracy
and a generalized dualism. He must condemn superficial
economism, which would modernize the country and rationalize society by constructing factories with another's money,
another's technology, another's administration. When it
comes to the problems of minorities and local democracy, he
must cease from censoring himself for fear of imperiling an
apparent national unity. The Arab revolutionary intellectual
has too long applauded the call to Arab unity, the while
accepting and sometimes justifying the fragmentation that is
reality.

Everyone subscribes to a unity founded on feelings; a unity

11. E.g., the Pharaonic ideology of Dr. Husain Fawzi, *Sindbad
égyptien* (in Arabic), *op. cit.* The book is nonetheless a worthy
experiment in psychological history.

founded on economy is condemned as being too slow to transpire. There are those who prefer to panegyrize Arab unity rather than bring it about. Only an historical critique can put an end to such seductions.

This critique must be carried out on two levels: first, the Arab states, within those territorial organizations to which each revolutionary intellectual belongs. Second, the Arab unitary movement: this must be structured, liberated from every consideration of or dependence on local interests, freed from the limitations of current political practice, and given the major role of criticizing and evaluating the actions, organizations, and policies of the Arab states insofar as they influence the future of the Arabs. Thus will it safeguard the rights of the future as revealed by positive analysis, recalling always the shared interests of the community whenever the tendency to consider local, sectional, and transitory interests threatens to gain the upper hand.

Necessarily assuming many forms, this labor will in any case accomplish the modernization of Arab society, whatever the ultimate result of the unitary movement in which victory or failure is assured to nobody.

Today, outside his personal successes the Arab revolutionary intellectual must lead an unhappy life, because his society is living in an infrahistorical rhythm. He will not put an end to his anguish until he clearly expresses what he knows to be the prerequisites for radical renovation and then defends them with all his strength, thus bringing finally to a close the long winter of the Arabs.

GLOSSARY

adab	A genre of literature; "belles-lettres."
akhbār	Narrations of incidents in early Islamic history.
ʿAlawites	The dynasty reigning in Morocco since the early seventeenth century.
ʿAlīds	Descendants of ʿAlī, the Prophet's son-in-law.
Almohads [Almohades]	Muslim dynasty founded in North Africa in the twelfth century.
amīn (lit. trustworthy)	An attribute of the Prophet.
asāṭīr	Legends, myths.
ʿaqīda	Creed or dogma.
Brahmo Samaj	A reformist movement initiated in nineteenth-century Bengal by Raja Ram Mohan Roy.
dīwān	An institution in the Islamic caliphate dealing with public registers of receipts and expenditures; also a warehouse or exchange, synonymous with caravanserai.
faqīhs	Experts in Islamic jurisprudence.
Fāṭimīds	A Muslim dynasty of the Ismāʿīlī Shīʿas founded in the tenth century. Their name refers to the descent which they claimed from ʿAlī, the Prophet's son-in-law, and Fāṭima, the Prophet's daughter.
fiqh	Islamic jurisprudence.
Futūḥāt	Refers to the book *Futūḥāt al-Shām* ("The Conquests of Syria") written by al-Baladhūrī, the great Arab historian of the ninth century.

178

ghayb	Hiden or Unseen Realm; the state of concealment of the Divine Essence.
Ibāḍism	A sect in North Africa generally thought to be an offspring of the Khārijites, an early movement of dissent.
igmāᶜ	Consensus of the learned (literally, agreeing upon); one of the four basic principles from which Muslim law is derived.
Ism	A divine name.
kaids	Tribal chiefs in Morocco.
kalām	Muslim theology.
kalamulujiya	Logomachy.
Kāmil	Refers to the title of a book, *al-Kāmil fīʾl-Tārīkh*, by ᶜIzz al-Dīn Abu l-Ḥasan ᶜAlī b. al-Athīr (1160-1233), the highpoint of Muslim annalist historiography.
khatībs	Spokesman of a tribe; also one who delivers a sermon at the Friday prayer.
Maghāzī	Refers to *Kitāb al-Maghāzī* ("The Book of Campaigns"), by Abu ᶜAbd Allāh Muhammad b. ᶜUmar al-Wāqidī, a noted Arab historian of the second century of the Muslim era.
Fātimīd Maḥdī	ᶜUbayd Allāh, the first Fātimīd caliph (909-934).
Mahdism	Islamic counterpart of the Judeo-Christian concept of the Savior or Messiah.
Makhzen	Politico-military elite in Morocco.
Maraboutism	The "saint cult" in North Africa.
Mashriq	Arab countries east of the Maghrib.
mihnah	The inquisition established by the ᶜAbbāsīd caliph al-Maʾmūn to enforce conformity to Muᶜtazilite doctrine.
Minhāj al-Sunna	Title of a book by al-Ghazālī (1058-1111), one of the most original thinkers of Islam and its greatest theologian.
munāẓara	Religious debate.
mutakallimūn	Theologians.

Naḥda	Literary renaissance of the Arabs in the nineteenth century.
naḥw	Grammar.
salafī	Those who espouse the earliest form of Islam as practiced by the Prophet and the four rightly-guided caliphs.
Sanusiiyya movement	A Ṣūfī order that originated in Algeria, whence it came to Libya in the nineteenth century.
Second Naḥda	A movement of Arab reassertion and self-examination in the mid-1960s.
shaykhs	Elders in general; Ṣūfī elders in particular.
shūra	Consultation as a political principle.
sunna	The deeds, utterances, and unspoken approval of the Prophet.
Sunnī ʿaqīda	The sunnī creed; its followers refrain from deviation in dogma and practice.
Ṭabaqāt	Refers to the book *Ṭabaqāt al-Ṣaḥāban* ("Classes of the Companions"), by Abu ʿAbd Allāh Muḥammad b. Saʿd (784-845), a traditionalist.
taḥaddī	Challenge.
tārīkh	History; historiography.
tathwīr	To revolutionize.
ʿulama	Religious scholars of Islam.
Usṭūrah	Legend; myth (pl. asāṭīr).